A HANDBOOK for PARENTS

ALICE FRYLING
ROBERT FRYLING

Foreword by
Larry Crabb

INTERVARSITY PRESS
DOWNERS GROVE, ILLINOIS 60515

InterVarsity Press is the book-publishing division of InterVarsity Christian Fellowship, a student movement active on campus at hundreds of universities, colleges and schools of nursing in the United States of America, and a member movement of the International Fellowship of Evangelical Students. For information about local and regional activities, write Public Relations Dept., InterVarsity Christian Fellowship, 6400 Schroeder Rd., P.O. Box 7895, Madison, WI 53707-7895.

All Scripture quotations, unless otherwise indicated, are from the Holy Bible, New International Version. Copyright © 1973, 1978, International Bible Society. Used by permission of Zondervan Bible Publishers.

Cover photograph: Michael Goss

ISBN 0-8308-1742-5

Printed in the United States of America ∞

Library of Congress Cataloging-in-Publication Data
Fryling, Alice.
    A handbook for parents/Alice Fryling and Robert Fryling;
foreword by Larry Crabb.
        p. cm.
    Includes bibliographical references.
    ISBN 0-8308-1742-5
    1. Family—Religious life.   2. Family.   3. Parenting—Religious
aspects—Christianity.   4. Family—Psychological aspects.
I. Fryling, Robert, 1947-   . II. Title.
BV4526.2.F7955   1991
248.8'45—dc20   91-21853
                                                                                 CIP

15   14   13   12   11   10   9   8   7   6   5   4   3   2   1
99   98   97   96   95   94   93   92   91

Foreword

Christian people who write about parenting sometimes tend either to overspiritualize and oversimplify or, perhaps unwittingly, to secularize the process. The first group treats the Bible as if it were reducible to a step-by-step set of instructions for assembling a lovable child. The second misses the depth of the struggle facing anyone who wants to be an instrument of blessing in a loved one's life, a struggle with self-centeredness and immaturity that will be fully resolved only in eternity.

Realism requires we admit that life, for sometimes long seasons, can be an unsatisfying mess. Faith enables us (not easily, quickly or every time) to handle our lives with joy and confidence in a God whose faithfulness often operates out of our sight until the eternal day when he fully reveals to us just how true Romans 8:28 really is.

Realism and *faith:* those are the two words that come to mind as I read the Frylings' book on parenting. It is a realistic book that builds on faith without overspiritualizing. It offers practical advice without suggesting that parenting can be adequately described in doable activities. And it highlights the essential truth that, above all, parenting is building a relationship characterized by sacrificial commitment, humbling honesty and true affection.

Nothing presents a less biblical view of things than a description of always-loving, rarely-failing people who get along wonderfully all the time. Bob and Alice reflect the realism of Scripture without losing sight of the possibilities of faith. You don't get the feel from reading their book that they are perfect parents. Nobody is! But I believe (from personal knowledge and from the book) that they are *good* parents who deeply love their kids and who, because they wrestle honestly with the difficult parts of parenting, have something to say.

And they say it well, with humor, integrity and insight. This book is not really a handbook in the usual sense of that word. There are no sure-fire formulas here. If there were, I'd throw the book away. But there are discerning observations from committed, caring parents who have learned to *think biblically* about raising children in the midst of busy lives. Their thoughts are worth reading.

You'll come away from this book more accepting of your weaknesses, more devoted to your kids and more eager to trust the Lord in the adventure of parenting.

Dr. Lawrence J. Crabb, Jr.

Introduction

The title is important. This book is not called *How to Be a Great Parent*. I don't even *know* any parents who are great all the time.

It is not called *Problem Solving for 20th-Century Parents*. Our children are not problems to be solved but people to be loved.

And it is not called *Ten Easy Steps to Better Parenting*. Rarely, if ever, have I taken a step toward "better parenting" which has been easy. The steps I have taken have usually been faltering, sometimes painful, often slow and difficult.

Becoming a better parent frequently means giving up something I cherish: my time, my affections, my selfish goals or my own limited expectations. I have never found overcoming selfishness easy. Nor have I found parenting easy. In fact, I do not have any friends who consider their jobs as parents "easy."

Easy, no. But rewarding, yes. Parenting is by far the most challenging, satisfying and rewarding job I have ever done. I did not come into marriage eager to have a whole bevy of little Frylings. My training was with college students. I wasn't sure I would know what to do with my own children for the first eighteen years. I wasn't sure I would like dirty diapers (I didn't), constant responsibility (I flinched) or endless rounds of playing Candyland (I cheated).

What a surprise to find out that even though I didn't like those things, I loved being a parent. I love the creativity of parenting. I love the curiosity of my daughters. I love watching them blossom. I love their questions. I love their answers! I love my children.

But my love for Dorie and Elisa does not automatically make me a good parent. Frustration, confusion and pain have made me a good parent. "Suffering produces perseverance; perseverance, character; and character, hope. And hope does not disappoint us" (Rom 5:3-5). Being honest about my needs, asking questions, sharing my successes and failures with my husband and my close friends is the *modus operandi* of my parenting experience.

I was still getting used to the surprise of enjoying my children as much as I do (and it has gotten better every year) when I hit another more recent surprise in a different area of my life. For over twenty years, Bob and I have been working with InterVarsity Christian Fellowship. When I started meeting with students in 1966, they considered me a peer. Now, much to my surprise, many students look to me as a substitute mother. Many of the students we meet come from broken homes, dysfunctional families or absentee parents. Many are victims of emotional, verbal or sexual abuse. For some, I was one of the first "older" Christian women who showed interest in them. They drank it up.

And they began to tell me I should write a book about parenting— not because they had seen faultless ability on my part, but because they saw me struggling with family issues that they wished their parents had addressed.

As we talked about the daily difficulties in their lives, we talked about mothers, fathers, brothers, sisters and friends. We talked about relationships, ideas and values that should have been part of their childhood experiences but were not. Now these young people were adults, almost ready to become parents themselves, and yet they still needed to ask questions, test answers and experience the unconditional love of a parent.

And so the idea they planted began to grow in my brain. Perhaps I could write a book which would help these student friends as they became parents. Perhaps I could write a book which would help my friends and me continue the job we began so innocently years ago. As I began to think of the book as a "handbook" rather than a "textbook," its appeal grew for me.

But I had one more hurdle to overcome. If I were a teenager, I would have serious reservations about my parents writing a book about parenting. Dorie and Elisa know better than anyone else that we are not an ideal family. I wondered if they would even consider letting me take on this new venture.

But I underestimated their generosity and their love for me. They both enthusiastically encouraged me to try it. (I did, of course, give them veto rights over all stories and illustrations!)

Bob was equally enthusiastic. I tend to be the self-appointed scribe in our family when we take on jobs like this, but the ideas, perspectives and experiences come from both of us. So, even though I write in the first person, I am asking InterVarsity Press to consider us both the authors. Bob has given me much more than my children. He is an outstanding example of the truth that "the best thing a father can do for his children is to love their mother." My life as a parent, as a person, as a child of God is richer and more complete because of Bob's love for me. Up until the point of actually putting words in sentences, Bob is very much the co-author of this book.

When I sat down to outline what I would say in a book about parenting, I found myself thinking in terms of relationships and communication more than the "how-to's" of discipline. Disciplining our children is, of course, an important part of parenting. But I do not think it is the best place to begin.

I remember one time when Dorie, at about two-and-a-half, stubbornly refused to leave her friend's home where she had been playing. I found myself between a rock and a hard place. Should I exercise authority and spank her? Or should I argue and harass until one of us gave in?

We certainly can't say ahead of time exactly what to do in every situation. But we can learn how to build relationships within the family which will weather the storms of these questions and sustain love even when we fail.

Yesterday our pastor made the observation that the job of the church is to "teach people *how* to think rather than tell people *what* to think." I hope this book will help you grow in learning *how* to think about parenting, so that when you need to decide *what* to say or do, you will have many reference points to guide you.

As you work through this handbook, please do not consider the first half of each chapter the most important part. The most important part is, by far, the part *you* write as you answer the questions. The best way to do this will be to answer them on your own and then share your answers with your spouse. If you are a single parent, look for a close friend, perhaps another single parent, who can share the answers to the questions with you. If you are parenting a blended family, you may want to amplify the questions to include your special needs, but most of the questions can be answered in light of the current family you are creating. I have also included questions for small groups which can be used after the more personal questions have been answered.

God bless you as you live out the image of the Creator, both as his child and as a parent to the children he has given you.

Alice Fryling

Chapter 1
Why Families?

"I'm a failure as a parent. When I hear about all the dumb things parents do to their kids, I think of myself and say, 'GUILTY!' I feel so bad to think I have messed up my children's lives. I don't know how I can ever correct all the mistakes I've made."—a discouraged parent

It might sound as if those words were spoken by a parent who grew up in an abusive home. Perhaps someone who was converted later in life, someone who had little relational or spiritual training. I'd like to say that this person had no role models and few opportunities to learn how to be a good parent. What more could you expect from a person like that?

That's what I'd like to tell you. But those words are from the journal of someone who should know better. She has had good role models. She has had many opportunities to learn. In fact, some people mistakenly think she is a wonderful parent. But I know better. Those words are a paraphrase from my own diary.

One of the great disappointments of my life is that I am not the wonderful, consistent, wise parent I would like to be. The day I wrote those words in my journal, I felt overwhelmed by the deep, painful reality of my inadequacies, my selfishness and my weaknesses as a mother.

It was a day when I wondered whether God had made a mistake when he gave me children. And I know other parents who have felt the same way.

In fact, considering the high risk of failure, it is a legitimate question to ask, "Why in the world does the Creator God allow helpless babies to grow up in families?" There is a divine absurdity in the idea that a sinful man and woman be given responsibility for the spiritual, social, intellectual and emotional training of a child. Add into the picture a second or third child, and the potential for sin is multiplied.

True, the helpless baby needs physical care. But animals care for their young without the risk of damaging them by their own moral sinfulness. Perhaps, after all, there would be a better way to raise children than in families. Might there be an environment where a child could mature to adulthood without being impacted by the selfishness and pride of their parents and siblings?

Perhaps there could be another way. But evidence is that our Creator decided that the value of family relationships was worth the risk of failure. In fact, families are not a mistake at all, but a planned part of creation. When the first man, Adam, lived in the garden, he was surrounded by all kinds of animals and plants. He even had a perfect relationship with God, untainted by sin. But God looked at his life and said, "It is not good for the man to be alone" (Gen 2:18). Adam needed relationship with other human beings. He needed a wife. So God made a woman and brought her to Adam—and thus the first family unit was formed.

From that union came hundreds and hundreds of families which eventually made up the nation of Israel. The Old Testament tells the history of God's people by describing them in their family units. Almost every book of the Old Testament mentions families. In the New Testament, the significance of families is reinforced when the Lord declares that those of us who are believers are all in one family (Eph 3:15; Heb 2:11).

We can assume, therefore, that families were not an afterthought, invented because God couldn't think of anything else to do with babies and children. No, God placed children in families because families are good places to be. God intends for families to be places where children will be safe from physical danger, and also safe to experiment with life as they find out who they are and what adulthood looks like. Families, furthermore, have a spiritual dimension which goes far beyond the feeding of babies and the raising of children.

The family unit is, first of all, a metaphor of life's greatest spiritual reality: God Is. God exists. God is the great "I Am." His existence is the basis for all other existence. And his existence is described as a Trinity: the Father, the Son and the Holy Spirit. In other words, God exists in relationship with himself. And part of who he is is best described using the family terms *father* and *son*. Scripture persistently describes God in family terminology. God is called mother: "As a mother comforts her child, so I will comfort you" (Is 66:13). God's children are not only called sons, but also daughters: "Sing, O Daughter of Zion; shout aloud, O Israel! Be glad and rejoice with all your heart, O Daughter of Jerusalem!" (Zeph 3:14). Jesus called those who believe in him his brothers and sisters (Mk 3:35).

Mother, Father, Son, Daughter, Brother, Sister. All these words describe the God who is, and his relationship to his people. So when you and I struggle to know who we are as mothers and fathers, as sons and daughters, as brothers and sisters, we are also struggling to know more about what God is like. As a human father learns how to love his children, he is also learning how God loves him. And as a mother learns to give grace and forgiveness to her children, she also grows in her appreciation of the grace and forgiveness of God.

No, families are not an afterthought. They are an illustration of the God who has always existed, first in relationship with himself and then in relationship with his people. But families are more than a metaphor. They are also a gift. "God sets the lonely in families" (Ps 68:6). "Sons are a heritage from the LORD, children a reward from him" (Ps 127:3). Families are God's gift to us, not merely to meet our needs for companionship but also to provide an environment for spiritual growth. I like the American Standard Version of Judges 6:34 (margin): the Spirit of the Lord "clothed" himself in Gideon. I believe that the Spirit of the Lord is, likewise, "clothing" himself in me, in Bob, in Elisa and in Dorie. We learn from the Spirit in each of us. We are loved by the Spirit in each of us. We are growing closer to God, through his Spirit, within the context of our family relationships.

One of the first Bible passages we studied as a family was Deuteronomy 6:5-7: "Love the LORD your God with all your heart and with all your soul and with all your strength. These commandments that I give you today are to be upon your hearts. Impress them on your children. Talk about them when you sit at home and when you walk along the road, when you lie down and when you get up." For several weeks we had a little picture on our bulletin board of stick figures sitting and walking, lying down and getting up, talking about God's love.

It is one of our jobs as parents to "impress" our children with God's Word. It is also one of our jobs to pray for our children. Job got up early in the morning to offer sacrifices for each of his children. "Perhaps," he thought, "my children have sinned and cursed God in their hearts" (Job 1:5). So part of the gift God gives to children by placing them in families is the instruction and prayers of their parents.

Children are also very much a part of the spiritual growth process of their parents. In the early years of our family, I struggled to learn to be a mother. My patience frequently ran out before noon. But my anger seemed to flow out of endless reserves. Fatigue was a familiar enemy. I often thought of the punishment God declared to Eve for her sin in the garden: "With pain you will give birth to children" (Gen 3:16). The physical pain of labor and delivery was only a hint of the stress I would feel as I sought to continue the birth process in my children's emotional, social, and intellectual development. And I knew that my pain was indeed associated with that original "curse." Just as Adam and Eve's original sin was to live life their way instead of God's way, I knew that my own pain was often the result of my own willfulness and self-centeredness.

But I also had a sense that this pain was good for me. Dorie, our first-born, entered the world as a curious, eager little person who wanted to be involved in all aspects of life—my life. As Dorie and I got to know each other, I found that my love for independence, my craving for time alone, and my desire for order and predictability were in conflict with her needs, first just to be with me, and later, to question, talk about and evaluate all aspects of our life together. As much as I struggled with the frustration of growth (hers and mine), I soon realized that mothering Dorie was making me a better person. Her needs and demands were, in fact, sanctifying me. I found out that I could live life less independently and more generously, and that I could learn to be loving and flexible, even when that meant that my life could not be so orderly and predictable. These were things God wanted me to be learning.

I found comfort in the words Paul wrote to Timothy: "Women will be saved through childbearing—if they continue in faith, love and holiness with propriety" (1 Tim 2:15). This confusing verse has been subject to much theological debate, but one interpretation intrigues me. Perhaps, someone said to me, one assumption of that verse is that children have a way of pushing us to places that seem beyond our ability. Our children's needs often motivate us to overcome our bent to sin. Even sinful attitudes such as selfishness and pride can be overcome in unexpected ways by the demands of our children. God uses a variety of ways to bring sanctification into every life. Most mothers and fathers can attest to the fact that we have our children to thank for some of the victory over sin and other rough edges in our lives.

Families, then, are a wonderful idea. They illustrate the nature of God. They are God's gift to us. They are part of the process of our own spiritual growth, our own sanctification. At a time in history when the family is being severely threatened by new sociological norms, we need to remember its importance.

In her commencement address at Wellesley College in 1990, Barbara Bush, wife of the president of the United States, said, "At the end of your life, you will never regret not having passed one more test, winning one more verdict, closing one more deal. You will regret time not spent with a husband, a child, a friend or a parent. Our success as a society depends not on what happens in the White House but on what happens inside your house." This echoes what Scripture has been saying for centuries. Our obedience to God begins at home.

This book is an attempt to help us, as parents, be obedient to God the Father. The questions at the end of each chapter are intended to help you focus more clearly on your strengths and weaknesses in fulfilling your parenting responsibilities. We are not looking for fill-in-the-blank, right and wrong answers. As you think through your answers to each question, perhaps you will come to understand yourself better.

Self-awareness is often the first step to an awareness of God at work in our lives. As you discuss your answers with your spouse (or a close friend), you may begin to see a kaleidoscope of experiences and impressions which help make you who you are. And, if you choose to answer the questions for group discussion, you may learn new ideas from other parents and enhance your ability to parent your own children.

For Personal Reflection
1. Write down five adjectives that come to mind when you think of the words *mother* and *father.*
father:

mother:

Which of these adjectives accurately describe you? Which accurately describe God? What is your personal source for the negative ones? For the positive ones?

If your children are old enough, ask them to tell you five words which describe you. How do their lists compare with your lists?

2. List ten advantages you and your children have by being in your family.

(1)

(2)

(3)

(4)

(5)

(6)

(7)

(8)

(9)

(10)

3. In what ways do you experience "family relationships" with other believers (Heb 2:11)? What aspects of "family" do you wish you experienced more with other Christians?

Are there any parts of your experience in the Christian community which remind you of unhealthy family relationships?

4. Identify three major stress points for you as a parent. How might God use those stresses to help you grow spiritually or emotionally?

(1)

(2)

(3)

5. In Numbers 2:2, God, through Moses and Aaron, instructed the Israelites to gather around the Tent of Meeting in families, each one under "his standard with the banners of his family." If you were to make a banner depicting your own family, what symbols would be on it? (Some families have enjoyed actually making these banners out of paper or felt and then hanging them in a special place in the home.)

For Group Discussion
1. No family is perfect, but think of several families you know whose relationships seem to reflect, at least in some ways, the relationship God has with us. What are some of the qualities of these families? What are the fathers like? What are the mothers like? How do the children respond to their parents? What makes these families unique?

2. How has being a parent helped you to grow spiritually?

What is one of your main areas of growth right now that your children are influencing?

3. Describe your own father and mother. How did growing up in your family of origin help or hinder your view of God as a father and as a mother?

4. In 1 Chronicles 23, David gathered together the Israelites and gave them family "assignments" related to service in the temple of God. Can you identify an "assignment" God has given your family?

What gifts do you offer your friends, your church or your community? If you find it difficult to define your "assignment," ask someone who knows you well to answer this question for you.

Chapter 2
Family Language

Every family speaks its own language. It is a language spoken by no other family. It may be partly verbal, partly non-verbal: communicated by gestures, signs, facial expressions and tones of voice as well as by words. A family's language can be characterized by love, concern, anger, worry, criticism or a host of other attributes. Just as our American language is characterized by hundreds of idioms from other cultures, so our family's language is full of influences from the past—from our own parents, our spouse's family, and generations of grandparents, aunts and uncles.

Let me give you some examples of relational "language," of the kinds of signs and symbols that make up family language.

Soon after they were married, Bryan made up a song to sing to Ellen to the tune of "Why Do I Love You?" He has been singing it now for so many years that he can hum a few bars when Ellen seems to need encouragement, and she knows that he is saying, "I love you."

A few Sundays ago, Ellen had a difficult experience before church. As they sat down, Bryan tapped his finger on the pew to the rhythm of his song, and Ellen "heard" him saying, "I know this is difficult, but, remember, I love you!" Their marriage speaks the language of love.

In contrast, Sarah's family spoke a language of broken promises. When Sarah was in elementary school and high school, her mother's life was full of many activities and interests. That would have been fine except her mother "spoke" a language that communicated to Sarah that she was not a very important person. Even though her mother said she loved her, Sarah's memories include the innumerable times her mother would sail out the door to a meeting ("I'll be back in an hour") only to return four or five hours later full of apologies and excuses. As an adult, it has been hard for Sarah to feel loved and to trust other people. No wonder. The language she learned growing up was the language of broken promises.

Another family I know speaks the language of criticism. In this family nothing is ever quite good enough. A job well done is always seen as a job-that-could-have-been-done-better. In this family, criticism is not always communicated through words. Sometimes silence, or lack of affirmation, does the job.

In our family, we sometimes succumb to the language of analysis. We can talk anything into the ground. Sometimes we talk about problems and issues until we suffer from the paralysis of analysis!

Or there is the family whose language is the language of politeness. In this family everything is always "just fine." There are no overt disagreements or arguments. They pray together and play together, but they never fight together. It reminds me of the traveler's comment, "This is a nice place to visit, but I wouldn't want to live here." The reason I wouldn't want to live there is that the language of politeness is so unreal. It does not have words to describe the realities of sadness, disappointment or differences of opinion.

We need to be sure that our family language is a rich language, with words and expressions that describe the whole range of human experience. It needs to be a language that is truthful and free. Actually, truth and freedom usually go together. (See Jn 8:32 and 2 Cor 3:17.) A family that speaks the language of truth allows each family member to be free to express love, free to express disagreement, free to express a wide range of feelings.

I know of one mother who sat for almost half an hour with her daughter on her lap, listening to the young girl express her anger toward her friend Jeanette. "I hate her! I hate her! She is so mean! I'm never going to speak to her again!" They were hard words to hear. And the mother did not like them. If the family language had been one of politeness, she probably would have forbidden her daughter to talk like that.

But because the mother was committed to the language of truth, she let her daughter speak the truth she was feeling, knowing that it was also true that the daughter would forgive Jeanette and that the friendship would continue. As she listened, the mother remembered that God had listened to the psalmist ranting and raving. "If only you would slay the wicked, O God! . . . I have nothing but hatred for them; I count them my enemies" (Ps 139:19-22). God himself speaks the language of truth and allows us to speak truthfully.

Truth, love, freedom—these are the qualities that we would like to have characterize our family language. But the language of truth and love does not come naturally. Sometimes I feel as though I need to "translate" my own desires and impulses in order to speak the language of love and truth.

We live in a world where evil and deception run rampant. Jesus identified this evil in the person of Satan, saying that when Satan

lies, "he speaks his native language" (Jn 8:44). We have been so taint-
ed by this evil that we, too, have "taught our tongues to lie" (Jer 9:5).
It is hard to overstate the destruction brought on by this language
of lies. It distorts the truth about God. It distorts the truth about
ourselves. It distorts the truth about our children. When we believe
Satan's language of lies, we risk falling into despair. We risk reaching
for the wrong goal. And we risk succumbing to lies ourselves.

In contrast to Satan, God never, ever lies. Paul wrote to Titus about
"a faith and knowledge resting on the hope of eternal life, which
God, *who does not lie,* promised before the beginning of time" (Tit 1:2).
Balaam reminded Balak that "God is not a man, that he should lie,
nor a son of man, that he should change his mind. Does he speak and
then not act? Does he promise and not fulfill?" (Num 23:19). Samuel
told Saul, "He who is the Glory of Israel does not lie or change his
mind; for he is not a man, that he should change his mind" (1 Sam
15:29). Our lives, our parenting style, our ways of relating to our
world would be very different if we always remembered that God
speaks truth and that his promises are utterly trustworthy.

But I find it hard to remember that. In fact, Satan's deceitfulness
has so invaded my life that remembering to believe and to speak the
truth comes to me with much difficulty, much like speaking a second
language. That's because it *is* a second language.

My "native language," the one that comes most naturally, says
that God does not care about me. My native tongue says that my
own needs are the most important needs around, that my thoughts
are the most profound, and that my feelings are always accurate.
This is the language of lies.

A doctor friend of mine hears this language every day in her office.
As a pediatrician, Barb sees a wider cross-section of our society than
many of us have the opportunity to observe. What she sees is not
always encouraging. "I'm concerned," she wrote to me, "that to some

degree we are facing a new generation of parents who were perhaps
indulged; at least they suffered very little material need, perhaps even
school and work came fairly easily, and now they parent either self-
ishly and shortsightedly (peace at any price)—or they are persuaded
that children will be better people if we make life soft for them,
cushioning their experiences physically and emotionally."

Barb says that when children in her office cry out in protest "I
don't want to, I don't want to!" she can assume that "I don't want
to!" works at home. She says she also sees this at church, in homes,
and in lifestyle attitudes. I take seriously her words as an observer of
our society. Perhaps Satan's native language of lies is being spoken
today as the language of easy living, we-deserve-the-best, and let's-
have-peace-and-quiet-at-any-price.

In contrast, God's language, the language of love, is humble, not
self-seeking and not self-indulgent. It allows truth, but it does not
demand a platform for truth. It admits anger, but does not let anger
turn to bitterness. It is polite, but it is not false. We can hear what
this language sounds like when we read the Gospels, where Jesus
speaks it fluently. It is a language full of grace and truth. The language of love is, in fact, the full, rich, colorful language we all long
to speak.

Determine and discuss your own family language by answering
the following questions.

For Personal Reflection
1. In each section of the following chart, write down one or two
recent examples which you think typifies the way you or your
spouse (if you are married) relate to your children.

	You	Your Spouse
Actions		
Gestures or Expressions		
Words		

Looking over your chart, what "language" do you think you speak?

What language do you think your spouse speaks? (Single parents: What language do you think your child hears from your friends?)

2. If someone were visiting your home, how would he/she describe your family language? (If you have a very honest friend, ask that person.)

3. When you are tempted to speak the language of lies, how do you do it? In what manner do you most often subvert the truth? What truths or realities are most difficult for you to speak about?

4. While language is both verbal and non-verbal communication, James warns us that the tongue (verbal communication) is of utmost importance. (See Jas 3.) Which of the following adjectives best describe the words you use? Put an x by the ones that describe the way you talk to your spouse (or good friends) and an o by the way you talk to your children.

kind	truthful	insensitive	optimistic
patient	judgmental	forthright	peaceful
angry	caring	tentative	excited
loving	defensive	indifferent	unfocused
critical	sensitive	opinionated	hopeful
false	indirect	joyful	reserved
accepting	accusing	gentle	harsh
distracted	careless	attentive	cautious

What observations can you make about the way you talk to your spouse or friends? to your children? What would you like to change in the way you communicate with your family?

For Group Discussion

1. Think about your church or community. What relational language is most commonly spoken? Validate each other's answers.

2. How would you describe your own personal "native language"? Share your answers.

3. The prophet Isaiah said that God will speak to us: "Whether you turn to the right or to the left, your ears will hear a voice behind you, saying, 'This is the way; walk in it' " (Is 30:21). Most of us have not heard a physical voice, but we have sensed God "speaking" to us. What characterizes God's language to you?

How does he reassure you? rebuke you? redirect you?

In what ways do you imitate God in the ways you reassure, rebuke and redirect your children? In what ways do you wish you imitated God's language more?

4. Read Ephesians 4:29-32. What unwholesome talk is most apt to come out of your own mouth?

Do you need to confess any sin in this area?

What kind of talk is most helpful for you to hear from others when you need "building up"?

What are some things we can do to get rid of bitterness, rage and anger?

What is the most compassionate thing someone has done for you recently?

Chapter 3
How Do You Say "I Love You"?
Qualities of Life

It is coffee hour at church. The adults are hovering around the coffee pot exchanging pleasantries.

"How was your trip?" "We missed you at the social last week." "Oh, by the way, thanks for taking my Sunday-school class at the last minute like that. I tried to get a sub, but no one was available." "Are you going to the Christmas pageant? I hear it's going to be great this year."

Almost unnoticed, another sound penetrates the social chatter. Little feet running down the hall. It sounds like about three or four pairs of little feet. The murmur of smothered giggles joins the running feet. Several parents stop mid-sentence and cock their heads like deer, alert to danger.

Suddenly, around the corner comes one half of the four-and-five-year-old Sunday-school class. Three of the children dart behind their parents, other children's parents, any adult who seems to offer protection. The fourth child enters with a squirt gun. As children #1, 2 and 3 weave in and out among the adults balancing coffee cups, child #4 takes aim, misses and takes aim again. Just as his shot hits its mark, his parent arrives and confiscates the squirt gun.

The adult pleasantries resume. But listen to the unspoken thoughts that are interfering with the chatter:

"Oh, dear, there goes Shawn again. I do wish his mother would keep him under control."

"Good grief! When I have kids, I'm not going to let them do that!"

"Isn't it wonderful that children can have fun in church? God's house belongs to people of all ages."

"Now what do I do? I hate to make a scene disciplining my child in church, but what do people think of me?"

This scenario, with endless variations, is repeated week after week in churches around the country as Christian parents take their children to worship God and to learn the tenets of their faith. We get our children ironed, ruffled, tied, polished and piled into the car. Then when we finally get to church, we find ourselves face to face with the same questions that haunted us all week. How do we train our children in "the way they should go"? How do we fulfill our God-given responsibilities as parents? What are those responsibilities, anyway?

Solomon's words are familiar to most parents: "Train a child in the way he should go, and when he is old he will not turn from it" (Prov 22:6). But what these words mean is not easy to determine. Is the proverb a command to be obeyed or an observation to be noted?

Perhaps the verse means, as John Charles Ryle writes, that parents should "remember that children are born with a decided bias towards evil, and therefore if you let them choose for themselves, they are certain to choose wrong" *(The Duties of Parents,* Christian Heritage Publishers, 1983, p. 3). Or Charles Swindoll may be more accurate when he says that "a child who is properly trained is trained in keeping with his or her own way, *not our way,* parents." "The verse," Swindoll writes, "is not just referring to the ultimate goal of bringing a child into right relationship with God and ultimately into a happy and prosperous future. It refers to the make-up of a child—his unique characteristics and mannerisms, which Scripture calls, 'his way' " *(Discipleship Journal,* 47, 1988, p. 28). How do we "train"? What is "the way"? How can we be "responsible Christian parents"?

I have been a parent for almost eighteen years, and I still do not know the answers to these questions. Sometimes Proverbs 22:6 has been a source of tremendous encouragement to me: yes, indeed, my kids will "turn out" okay. Sometimes it has been a source of rebuke to me: I have neglected my job of training. Over the years, the Spirit of God has whispered a variety of verses to my heart, applying them in different ways, depending on what I needed to hear. But as I muse on the one truth that has been woven throughout the words of encouragement, rebuke and guidance, it is that the greatest thing to learn is *to love.*

"If I have the wisdom of John Charles Ryle and Chuck Swindoll combined, but have not love, I am nothing. If I know how to meet every emergency, but have not love, I am empty. Knowledge, wisdom and instruction will always fail at some point. But love never fails." (See 1 Cor 13.)

Unfortunately, however, love does not always come easily to me. I have been highly influenced by Satan's native language of lies (selfishness, pride, unlove). Like many parents, I may feel love but have a hard time saying it. Or I may say it, and my children may have a hard time feeling it. But the essence of the gospel is *love.* It is not training. It is not rules. It is not even theology. It is love. God himself is love (1 Jn 4:16). The greatest gift we can give our children is to help them get to know this God who is Love. And they meet God first through us. Learning to say "I love you" to our children is perhaps our most important job as parents.

Look with me first at the qualities of life which communicate "I love you." Then we will look at what actions help those words to be effective. First, the qualities. The three characteristics which best communicate love within a family are grace, truth and faith.

Grace

I experience God's love in a variety of ways, but the most frequent and personal manifestation of his love is his grace. His grace is behind his forgiveness. God knows all of my thoughts, all of my actions, all of my intentions. He sifts out those which are selfish, boastful, hateful and harmful. And—he forgives me. In a similar way, we know our children better than anyone else does. We know how very much they need grace. Their experience of forgiveness begins at home. I like Daniel Taylor's observation: "One definition of 'home' is the place where you can be a complete jerk and they will still call you for dinner" (*Letters to My Children,* IVP, 1989, p. 111).

It is more than coincidence that Jesus' most famous parable about forgiveness takes place in the family. In the familiar story of the prodigal son (Lk 15:11-31), the father runs out to meet his wayward son, throws his arms around him, kisses him, then celebrates his son's return with a party. When I sin, and I forget that God is like that gracious father, I find myself cowering in fear. I picture God saying to me, "How *could* you? Didn't you know any better? You may come home, but you'll have to live in the barn until you pay for the damage you have done." Instead, the truth is that God is standing in the road, waiting for me with open arms.

Likewise, we need to welcome our children. One of the best ways we can say "I love you" is to greet failure with generous, nonjudgmental forgiveness.

The other day I walked into Janet's home, where I meet weekly with five other women for Bible study and support. The strong smell of fresh paint greeted me just inside the front door. Janet told us that the fresh paint was not on their bathroom walls where it belonged, but on the carpeted steps going upstairs to the bathroom.

The unopened can of paint had been at the top of the stairs the day before. Janet's son, Chris, had been horsing around in the upstairs hallway. Suddenly the can of paint bounced off the top step and tumbled all the way to the bottom step, opening its lid on the way and spewing out its oil-based, promise-to-cover-everything contents. Chris, of course, screamed in dismay. Janet ran for the mop, the pail, anything which had the potential to remove oil from a carpet.

When I asked Janet if she punished Chris, she said, "Oh no, he scolded himself enough without my adding to it." Chris helped clean up the mess, and he and Janet talked about what happened, but Janet wisely realized that in the end Chris needed grace, not punishment.

After we had all had a good laugh at Janet's description of the mess, we talked about *grace* between parents and children. Is it easier to extend grace in big things or little things? Is there potential for too much grace? What does grace look like to a toddler? To a teen? When is grace freely given and when is it spoiled by conditions attached to it?

All the women in our group are mothers. These are not theoretical questions. We all want our children to grow up in an atmosphere of grace, where they can learn to know the God who loves them, forgives them and is gracious toward them. We need grace to be able to do that.

Truth

Another quality of life which will help communicate "I love you" is truthfulness. In fact, grace and truthfulness go hand in hand. Jesus,

God in the flesh, came in grace and truth (Jn 1:14). The truth is that God exists, that God is holy, and that we are not. Grace is God's response to that truth. This give me freedom to be truthful about my own needs and weaknesses and about my children's needs and weaknesses.

The loving parent can truthfully say, "I was wrong." The loving parent can truthfully say, "You were wrong." Parent and child alike can be truthful about their desires, their questions and their fears. Children who can come to their parents and truthfully confess both their strengths and their sins, their thoughts and their ideas, and know that they will be received with grace—those are children who are loved.

A loving parent gives truthful feedback to his children. Children need to learn that they are sinners, saved by grace. They need to learn that their own desires cannot always take precedence over other people's needs and desires. They need to learn patience, self-control and active obedience. But they also need to learn the good truth about themselves. When Jesus was baptized, the Father said to him, "You are my Son, whom I love; with you I am well pleased" (Mk 1:11). I hope Dorie and Elisa's memories of their childhood include many times when Bob and I have said, "With *you* we are pleased!"

Many parents are so intent on making sure that their children are "humble" that they forget to affirm and build up. Life brings its own humbling experiences. Home, on the other hand, is where we can find refuge from some of the painful experiences that humble us. The concept of home is a rich and meaningful one in Scripture. Listen to what Henri Nouwen says about our spiritual "home":

> The home, the intimate place, the place of true belonging, is therefore not a place made by human hands. . . . Words for "home" are often used in the Old and New Testaments. The Psalms are filled with a yearning to dwell in the house of God, to take refuge under

God's wings, and to find protection in God's holy temple; they praise God's holy place. . . . Jesus reveals himself as the new home: "Make your home in me, as I make mine in you" (Jn 15:4). *(Life-signs,* Doubleday, 1986, pp. 36-37)

Once again, the family becomes a metaphor for human beings' relationship with God. Our homes become symbols of the place of truth and grace where God accepts us, affirms us and loves us.

Faith

A third quality of life which fosters an environment where love can be experienced is faith. I am free to love my children because I believe that God is with us. If God were not with us, then I would have to prove my love, justify my failures and manipulate my children. But even in the most stressful times of family life, *God is with us.* I learned from the Israelites how important it is to remember to have faith in this truth.

When the people of Israel left Egypt, they left in the midst of great miracles and manifestations of God's power. If anyone had reason to believe in God and his care, the Israelites did.

But look at what happened just a few miles into the desert. They started to complain. They quarreled. They grumbled. Worse yet, they tested God (Ex 17:1-7). That made him angry (Ps 95:10). Do you know what they said that made God so angry? It wasn't just that they complained about their living conditions. It was, specifically, that they questioned whether God was with them. "Is the Lord among us or not?" they asked.

What a lesson for Christian parents! When the going gets rough, when things seem hopeless, when we can't see how we will make it, we dare not challenge God by giving into the fear that he is no longer with us. When my family experiences quarrels, complaints and grumbling, I am tempted to react in despair. I fear that we have really done it this time. I fear we are beyond God's help. But that is a lie. It is a big lie. God is *always* with us. God is *always* redeeming. There is no sin, no mistake, no poor judgment that is beyond God's grace. When I settle down and translate the lie into the truth, and I remember that God is with us and will help us, then I almost always want to run to my family and say, "Oh, I love you!"

I am not always sure why the truth of God's presence generates love in my heart (and mouth and actions). It is probably because his presence gives hope—and hope frees me to love again. And it is probably because God is, indeed, love.

In the next chapter, we will look at how to say "I love you" with our actions. In the meantime, consider the following questions.

For Personal Reflection

1. What do you see as your most important job as a parent?

2. Think of someone who really loves you. What is it in that person's attitude that communicates this love?

3. 1 John 1:8-9 reads: "If we claim to be without sin, we deceive ourselves and the truth is not in us. If we confess our sins, he is faithful and just and will forgive us our sins and purify us from all unrighteousness."

Describe one time recently when you have experienced forgiveness:

between you and God:

between you and your spouse or a friend:

between you and your children:

Rewrite 1 John 1:8-9 in your own words and in the first person so that it describes one of these experiences of forgiveness.

4. Why do you think grace and truth go together? (What is it about grace that helps you be truthful? What is it about truth that helps you experience grace?)

In what situation recently have your children experienced grace and truth in you?

5. Write out one sentence stating a truth about God which helps you love your children more.

For Group Discussion
1. What quality of life in your family seems to be most helpful in communicating "I love you" to your children?

2. Think of an incident in your childhood when you felt forgiven. What happened?

3. How do you define grace?

Describe a recent situation where you saw grace exhibited in a human relationship.

4. Read Exodus 17:1-7 and Psalm 95. If you had been an Israelite in the desert, what three things would you have been most likely to complain about? What do those complaints tell you about yourself?

(1)

(2)

(3)

5. Think of a recent experience in your family which strengthened your own faith in the God who is with us. What happened and why was your faith strengthened?

How does your spouse (or a friend) encourage you best when you feel hopeless?

Chapter 4
How Do You Say "I Love You"?
Love in Action

Shortly after she delivered her first child, Julie had "a little talk" with the pediatrician. The doctor gave her this bit of advice: "You will hear all kind of things about how to care for your baby. Your next-door neighbor and your Great-Aunt Tilly will give you more suggestions than you know what to do with. Friends will give you books. Other people will give you magazines. My advice to you is to pick one author, and let that person be your authority. Pick your author well, but then don't be confused by the multitude of choices."

If I had the opportunity to recommend only one book, besides the Bible, to new parents, it would be Ross Campbell's book *How to Really Love Your Child* (Victor Books, 1977). In fact, since I first read the book twelve years ago, I have purchased well over a hundred copies to give to friends and acquaintances. (I guess I'm the kind of friend the good doctor was describing!) The reason I like Campbell's book so much is that he addresses the question of *why children of loving parents sometimes do not feel loved.*

A friend of mine had this to say after she looked through a group of her baby pictures: "I was surprised at how cute I was as a little girl. I wished I could go inside the picture and hug her and tell her so." What she probably really wished was that she could remember her parents hugging her and saying, "I love you so much, you cute little girl!"

It wasn't that my friend's parents didn't love her. They did. But somehow their love didn't register. Somehow she went all the way through her childhood, her teenage years, and on into her adult life feeling unlovely. What a tragedy. It is a tragedy of love lost. Love was lost, not because it wasn't there, but because it wasn't absorbed.

Campbell says that every child is asking the question "Do you love me?" "A child," writes Campbell, "asks this emotional question mostly in his behavior, seldom verbally. The answer to this question is absolutely the most important thing in any child's life." Campbell goes on to point out that most parents do love their children. "The feeling of love for a child in our heart may be strong. But it is not enough. By our behavior does a child see our love for him" (p. 32).

What kind of behavior, then, will communicate love? What can we *do* to say "I love you"? At this point, Campbell does not succumb to specifics: "If a child brings a squirt gun to church, here are the three things every responsible parent should do." Instead, he talks about giving the child eye contact, physical contact, focused attention and discipline. Campbell says that when we look our child in the eyes, when we give him or her lots of hugs and cuddles, when we spend time alone with our child, and when we carefully discipline, then our child will probably feel loved.

Perhaps because I have always been a busy person, with a big agenda for every day, what I needed to hear the most was his advice about focused attention. As a young mother, I quickly learned that one of my most precious commodities was my time. I seemed to have plenty of hugs and kisses. I knew how important it was to get down to a child's level and have good eye contact. But to give up a morning to "waste" time playing games was another story.

I remember when Dorie was still less than a year old, I read in my devotions the parable of the talents. Three men had been given talents (money) from their master to use while he was out of town. Two of the three invested the money and increased its value. The third buried his money out of fear. The master rebuked the third severely. His rebuke was a rebuke to me. "Is there anything you want me to do, Lord, with my time and energy (my abilities, my money) which I am not already doing?" His answer to me was clear: invest in your children.

God's word to me that day was that I needed to place a high priority on my time with Dorie, and later with Elisa. I needed to look at the time as an investment, with returns that I would only see later. A businessman would not consider a ten- or fifteen-year investment of his money a waste. In fact, many large financial investments take longer than that to appreciate. Looking at it that way, our ten or fifteen years of heavy time involvement with our children seems reasonable indeed. And any parent can tell you that the amount of time we invest in our children decreases as the years go on. Today, with both of our daughters teenagers, we are reaping the benefits of endless hours spent in play, in conversation, in cuddles, in just being together when they were young.

Looking back over the years, I have a little more perspective on my successes and my failures. My successes were wonderful. Reading books together until we all had them memorized. Playing games together, first with the artificiality of pretended competition, then in earnest as my children grew old enough to win more often than not! Talking together, sometimes tediously, about every detail of the school day; and sometimes with excitement, eager to share in each other's adventures. It all took so much time. Hours and hours. But it was worth every minute.

As I think about my failures, I remember the third servant in Jesus' parable. He failed because he was afraid. I wonder how much fear has a part in my own failures. Do I fill my day with too many activities because I am afraid? Perhaps I am afraid I will fail, so I do many, many things, hoping that if I fail at one activity, I will succeed at another. Or is fear driving me to prove my worth to the people in my church or to my friends and neighbors? Perhaps I am even afraid of God. So I drive myself to prove how trustworthy I am, and in the flurry of activity created by this effort, I bury the very talents he has given me.

Fear, then, may contribute to the tragedy of love lost. Pride also contributes to that tragedy. Which sounds better: "Oh, I had such a busy morning—after I dropped the children off, I led a Bible study at church and then rushed off to my part-time job at the insurance company," or "I played Candyland and Chutes and Ladders for three hours this morning"? The pride behind our busyness is a deception of our Enemy.

Another factor in the Lost Love Tragedy is lack of courage and creativity. Every parent is unique. And every child is unique. It takes courage to be different. It takes creativity to figure out the very best ways to spend time with our children.

Dorie loved to sew with me. She learned her colors sorting buttons. She practiced numbers counting them.

Elisa would have none of it. She was my Candyland Kid. Later it was doughnuts and "coffee" at the local bakery.

Are buttons and doughnuts the keys to good parenting? Not at all. They just provided experiences that each of us enjoyed. It was my job to figure out what those mutual pleasures might be, not to worry if they were different from other families and not to assume that they were right for everyone.

The important thing is that each family member experience quality time with every other member of the family. This is true, first of all, for husband and wife. Bob and I have had traditions of reading in front of the fire, going for walks, eating out in restaurants and just sitting on the sofa and talking.

With our children this time has taken different forms. Sometimes focused attention meant letting one of them "help"—even though any parent knows that a job done with a young child's "help" takes twice as long as a job done alone. Sometimes it meant creating time with one child when the other was busy with something else. Elisa and I went to the library each week while Dorie was at her piano lesson. Dorie and I went to Burger King while Elisa had her nap.

As the children got older, I found it more and more important to get out of the house, away from my own distractions, in order to really focus on them and their issues. This became a more expensive proposition when they grew out of doughnuts and into sandwiches and French fries. It would have been cheaper to eat at home. But by going out and "renting" a table at a restaurant, we were gaining much more than the snack.

Not long ago I was talking with Amy, a college student who had not had times like that with her mother. The conversation reminded me how meaningful those times can be. We started out talking about stewardship and budgeting, but we ended up talking about love. I mentioned that sometimes the value of something is more than monetary. I told Amy about my practice of "renting" tables by eating out.

Then I told her about one time when we were tightening up our budget. "In the next two months," I announced to my family, "I don't want to have to buy anything that is not absolutely necessary!" With that warning ringing in their ears, Dorie and Elisa went on their way. Later, Elisa came to me and asked if that meant we could no longer go out for snacks. "Oh, no!" I said, "That's a non-negotiable!" In other words, the time together was more valuable than the money spent.

I thought I had made a good point about stewardship. But Amy's eyes filled with tears. Forget the discussion about money. She wanted to know what it was like for a mother and daughter to go out for snacks. "That's so nice," she told me, "that you want to spend time with your kids." I've never met Amy's mother, but she sounds like a lovely lady, and she is a leader in her church. But her love was lost on Amy because she failed to invest her *time* in the things that were important to her child as she was growing up.

As I have talked with dozens of college students and adults, I have become more and more convinced that this tragedy is widespread. To love people is to be *interested* in them. It is to give them our undivided attention, at least for a small portion of our day. It is to say to the one who is loved, "You are the most important person in my life at this moment. I would like to talk about what you want to talk about. I would like to listen to you. I would like to enjoy being with you."

So then, if love is our native language, we will, as Ross Campbell suggests, spend time with our children, giving them eye contact, hugging them, talking with them and playing with them. In this way we speak love to our children. In the same way that a "picture is worth a thousand words," so our loving actions are worth more to our children than any of our words. "Dear children," the apostle John wrote, "let us not love with words or tongue but with actions and in truth."

For Personal Reflection

1. What is the most difficult action of love for you to give to your children: eye contact, physical contact, focused attention, discipline?

What step could you take that would enable you to give this more readily?

2. Ask your family to help you fill in the chart on the next page. If your children are too young to answer, ask your spouse or a friend to make an intelligent guess.

How do you evaluate the information on your chart?

3. Write out a prayer, verbalizing your thoughts to God about how you would like to love your children with actions.

4. John, the apostle who talked so much about love, wrote these words: "Do not love the world or anything in the world. If anyone loves the world, the love of the Father is not in him. For everything

Minutes spent talking with this person each day:	My accounting	Their accounting
My Spouse		
Child #1		
Child #2		
Child #3		

in the world—the cravings of sinful man, the lust of his eyes and the boasting of what he has and does—comes not from the Father but from the world" (1 Jn 1:15-16). How do you define:
a. the cravings of sinful man:

b. the lust of his eyes:

c. the boasting of what he has and does:

Describe ways in which these things hinder your love relationship with your children:
a. cravings:

b. lust of the eyes:

c. boasting:

For Group Discussion
1. In your family, what are the favorite ways of giving and receiving the following (compare answers):
eye contact:

physical contact:

focused attention:

2. Read Hebrews 12:5-6. How is discipline a manifestation of love?

Describe a situation where you saw discipline and love in action together.

3. What action have you taken recently to say "I love you": To your spouse? How was it received?

To one of your children? How was it received?

What action has your spouse taken to say "I love you" to you?

How do your children let you know that they love you?

4. Why did John say that we love because God loved us first (1 Jn 4:19)? In what ways is it a parent's responsibility to initiate loving actions in a family?

Chapter 5
Who Is Sabotaging Our Family?

Very few, if any, parents do not love their children. Very few, if any, do not want their children to know that they are loved. Most of us desperately want to be good parents. But we are often like the father who brought his young son to Jesus (Mk 9:17-24).

The boy had lost his speech and suffered from violent seizures. The man had taken his son to Jesus' disciples, but they hadn't been able to help. Picture the desperation of the father. "Jesus, he has been like this since he was a child! We can't seem to do anything to help him! He has almost died many times. Please, Jesus! Have pity on us."

Jesus looked at the father and reminded him, "Everything is possible to him who believes."

In a similar way, when I look at our family and see areas where healing and growth are necessary, I believe Jesus is reminding me that I must have faith, I must believe and I must obey. Then I will be a better parent.

But then, like the father in the story, I look at Jesus and say, "Lord, I do believe; help me overcome my unbelief." "Lord," I say, "I do want to live righteously and unselfishly. I want to be able to keep my children. I do want to be a good parent. Help me! Please!"

But in my most honest moments, I must admit failure. Like Jesus' disciples, I have not been able to do what I have been taught to do. I have made most of the mistakes a parent could make. I have done some dumb things. In fact, "I don't understand what I do. For what I want to do, I do not do, but what I hate I do. I have the desire to do what is good, but I cannot carry it out. For what I do is not the good I want to do; no, the evil I do not want to do—this I keep on doing" (see Rom 7). I ask myself, "Why can't I be a better parent? Why can't I be the kind, wise and loving person that I want to be?"

These are questions most honest, conscientious parents have asked at some time, in some form. I would like to suggest that the answer lies in the recognition that we are engaged in a global and personal spiritual battle. The battle between good and evil, between love and unlove, takes place on many fronts. The Christian family is not immune to the damaging effects of the battle. In fact, the family may be one of the main places where the Enemy attacks.

Our Enemy has many names: sin, Satan, the Great Deceiver, the powers of this dark world, spiritual forces of evil. Whether your awareness is more of your own sin, or of sin personified in Satan, no one can successfully dispute that the job of parenting is part of a great spiritual war. At the beginning of the book of Job, the Lord asks Satan where he has been. Satan replies that he has been "roaming through the earth and going back and forth in it" (Job 1:6).

He is still roaming around today. And he is looking not only for evil people to do his evil work. I believe he is looking for good people, like good Christian parents, with weak spots in our hearts. He is looking for parents who will allow their own selfishness, fear or pride to shadow the love of God in their lives. He is looking for us, when in a weak moment we will believe his lies. He is looking for our children, and he is eager to keep them from climbing into the arms of Jesus.

Not long ago I talked with a college student who came from a highly dysfunctional family. As we talked, she shared her struggles to follow Christ and her depression over her failures. Driving home, I prayed for her. The picture that came to mind as I prayed was one of warfare. Then I sensed the reassuring words of Jesus, "Satan wants her, but she is mine."

Our children are, likewise, his. But they will not be fully adopted into God's family without protest. In spite of our best desires, our own sin will fight their spiritual adoption. In spite of our best efforts, our children's sin will also fight this process. When we gave birth to our children, we were entering into a war that has been going on for generations. In fact, some of our frustrations today are generations old. "For I the LORD your God am a jealous God, visiting the iniquity of the fathers upon the children to the third and fourth generation" (Deut 5:9 RSV). Sin has a way of reproducing itself from one generation to the next.

Psychologists today, whether they are believing Christians or not, have become increasingly aware that struggles within families are not merely the result of immediate problems. Augustus Napier, author of *The Fragile Bond,* writes, "We see that the excesses of this generation are often unconscious attempts to 'balance the books' on the prior generation's injustices. As we try to work out the pain and frustration of the past, we complicate the present" (p. x). Quite frankly, I think "complicate" is too nice a word to describe the struggles I have felt as a parent!

Rather than depressing me, all of this talk about warfare and struggles with sin (our own and our forefathers') encourages me. Recognizing that family relationships are among the hardest hit in the spiritual warfare explains why parenting sometimes overwhelms me. It explains why even "good" parents sometimes struggle with "bad" children. Thomas Fuller, a seventeenth-century English pastor, observed that in Old Testament times "Rehoboam begat Abia; that is, a bad father begat a bad son. Abia begat Asa; that is, a bad father a good son. Asa begat Jehoshaphat; that is a good father a good son. Jehoshaphat begat Joram; that is a good father a bad son" ("Good Thoughts in Bad Times," *Christianity Today,* March 15, 1985, p. 50).

Why does this happen? Why is it that even when we do our best, sometimes we fail? It is because "our struggle is not against flesh and blood, but . . . against the powers of this dark world and against the spiritual forces of evil in the heavenly realms" (Eph 6:12). The battle is beyond my comprehension and beyond my own abilities. This does not mean that I am free to abdicate responsibility, but it does mean that I need to acknowledge that there is much more going on here than I can really understand. I am humbled by the magnitude of the war.

It is supremely significant, however, that out of all those mixed-up families in the Old Testament came the Lord Jesus Christ. Each of the families observed by Fuller is part of the genealogy of God's Son. So even though I do not always understand, and I certainly do not win every skirmish in the war, I can take heart that God is sovereign and will fulfill his purposes for our family. Even though we have "good" days and "bad" days in our life together, the ultimate outcome is in God's hands.

Parenting is, of course, difficult and painful. It is painful because of our own sin and our own inadequacies. It is difficult because we are prisoners of war (Rom 7:23). We are hostages of sin; our lives are not "business as usual." The business of parenting is in the context of spiritual warfare. Our enemies are self-centeredness, jealousy, anger, competition and hundreds of other manifestations of sinfulness which I see both in myself and in my children.

It helps me to name my Enemy. The Enemy is not lack of love. I love my children dearly. It is not ignorance. I've read enough books and articles to fill a bookcase. Nor is it lack of motivation. There is nothing I wish for more than my children's well-being and spiritual vitality. No, my Enemy is the Great Deceiver, the Accuser, the Prince of Darkness.

Thomas Fuller came to the following conclusion from studying the genealogy of Jesus. "I see," he said, "that my father's piety cannot be handed on; that is bad news for me. But I also see that actual impiety is not always hereditary; that is good news for my son." Likewise, recognition of our condition as participants in a spiritual war is good news and bad news. The bad news is that we will have to work very hard to win. The good news is that, in the long run, the victory belongs to the Lord, who loves us and is watching over us.

We do not know precisely what the victory will look like. Nor can we audaciously claim to win every battle. But our confidence is in God, who has given us the victory that "overcomes the world" (1 Jn 5:4).

For Personal Reflection
1. What do you see as the five strongest influences on your family life right now?
(1)

(2)

(3)

(4)

(5)

In what ways might these influences be used by God, for good?

In what ways might these influences have a negative effect on you and your children?

2. As you think about yourself, what are your own best weapons in the war we are facing? What strengths do you have, as a parent, which can enrich your children's growth toward maturity?

What strengths does your spouse have? (Single parents: What strengths do your closest friends offer to your children?)

3. Exodus 20:20 reads, "Do not be afraid. God has come to test you, so that the fear of God will be with you to keep you from sinning." (1) What are the greatest tests you face as a parent?

(2) How might "the fear of God" keep you from failing these tests?

(3) Why do you think God tells us not to be afraid when we are tested?

(4) Is there any sin in your life which you need to confess right now?

For Group Discussion
1. Read Ephesians 6:10-18.
(1) In what ways do you see parenting as a struggle "not against flesh and blood, but against the rulers, against the authorities, against the powers of this dark world"?

(2) How can each part of the armor of God help you in parenting? What are some practical things you do to keep yourself clothed in this armor?

Truth:

Righteousness:

Readiness:

The gospel of peace:

Faith:

Salvation:

The Holy Spirit:

Prayer:

2. Deuteronomy 5:9 in the New International Version says that God will punish "the children for the sin of the fathers." Does this seem fair to you? Why do you think a God who is described elsewhere as just and loving would allow children to suffer for their parents' and grandparents' sins?

Deuteronomy 5:10 says that God shows "love to a thousand generations of those who love me and keep my commandments." What are the benefits of growing up in a home where Christian love abounds? How does spiritual obedience on the part of the parents affect their children?

What good things did you learn from your parents?

3. Moses told the Israelites—mothers, fathers and children—to "go up and take possession of it [the land] as the LORD, the God of your fathers, told you. Do not be afraid; do not be discouraged" (Deut 1:21). Write out a sentence that you think describes the Word of the Lord to you right now, concerning your job as a parent. (What is God urging you to claim, or "take possession of" by faith, for your family?)

What fears do you have about obeying that command?

What discourages you most as you attempt to obey? What encourages you most?

Pray for one another.

Chapter 6
Independence vs. Dependence

One night at dinner Bob was joking about how he had always wanted to marry someone who was independently wealthy. "Oh, well," he joked, "one out of two isn't bad!"

That's right. Wealthy I am not; independent I am. I love to solve problems. I love to take initiative. I love to create. I love to work on my own. Even though there is a danger of becoming *too* independent, basically I like my independence. And it is as much a part of my heritage as great wealth would be.

I remember my Easter hat in 1955. During my elementary school years the Easter Parade was an event, not a just marketing gimmick as it is today. We really did get a new outfit for Easter. When I was in kindergarten my outfit included a new hat. It was a straw hat, with a velvet ribbon circling the whole thing, between the brim and the bonnet. The ribbon ended in the back with a glorious bow. Pastel flowers covered the circle of ribbon. It was, as you can imagine, the most beautiful hat I'd ever seen.

And I wanted to wear my new hat to school. To wear it before Easter was, of course, a travesty of the rules of the parade. Besides that, the day I chose to wear the hat, the weatherman was predicting rain. But I *had* to wear it to school. I wouldn't take no for an answer.

My mother let me wear it.

And it rained.

That's all I remember about my Easter hat. I don't remember wearing it in the Easter Parade. I don't remember my mother's reprimanding me, or even saying, "I told you so." In fact, I don't even remember if the hat got wet. What I do remember is that *my mother let me make a choice.* It turned out to be a bad choice. But it was a good thing to be able to make it. That's what I remember.

If all of life's choices had to do with hats and rainy days, the issue of independence versus dependence would be a minor one for parents. But life is full of very serious choices. Our job as parents involves negotiating the process of moving our children from their early days, when we make virtually all of their decisions, to the time when they enter adulthood and make life's choices and decisions on their own.

Because change is usually painful, this process is often difficult for both children and parents. It is difficult for our children because it involves risks. Growing into independence means moving into unknown territory. It takes more courage than some children have. It means taking more responsibility than some children want to assume. And it assumes a willingness to face failure which many of us do not have even as adults.

But independence is also a difficult thing for parents.

True, some parents push their children so fast toward independence that the children hit adulthood feeling lonely and unloved. Those parents must learn the value of spending lots of time with their children, the need most children have for security, and the place of parental protection in a child's life—protection from physical harm and buffering from emotional pain.

But I think I am more typical in that I am a parent who struggles more with allowing too *little* independence in my children's lives rather than too *much*. Perhaps because of who I am, perhaps because of the societal influences on me, perhaps even because I love being a parent so much, I find it difficult to let my children go.

Please don't misunderstand me. I am talking about the subtleties of independence, not the broad, bold strokes of the issue. I am talking about taking too much control in little areas, about making too many of the choices in the gray areas, and about my difficulty in learning to trust my children's abilities and choices in new areas.

If I had been Mary, the mother of Jesus, I too would have worried when Jesus stayed behind at the Temple. "Why have you treated us like this?" his mother asked, "Your father and I have been anxiously searching for you" (Lk 2:48). I find it incredible, on the other hand, that Jochebed, the mother of Moses, could put her little three-month-old baby in a basket and float him on the river (Ex 2:1-10). And yet it was that act of letting go which saved Moses' life.

I am a parent, then, who needs to learn to let my children decide to stay behind in the temple. I need to be willing to "float them on the river" if that is what God calls me to do. Because I do not think I am unique in my need, I have decided to spend some time looking at the question of how we can lead our children from total dependence at birth to appropriate independence eighteen years later.

There are at least three reasons why it is difficult for me to let my children become independent: my fears, my exaggerated sense of responsibility and my need to be needed.

Fear is one of the biggest problems I face. It is a problem by itself, and it magnifies my difficulties in the other areas of independence. At the root of my fears for my children, I must admit, are several lies.

The lies I am tempted to believe include these:

I can control my children's lives.

My worry protects them from danger.

I love my children more than God loves them.

I know better than God what is good for them.

Lies. All lies. It is a point of spiritual warfare for me to face these lies with faith and learn to believe the truth that God loves us and desires good for us. When I do well in the battle, I allow my children appropriate independence. When I lose a battle, then I waste energy and emotion in unproductive worry and I bind my children to me in unhealthy ways.

Scripture, on the other hand, teaches that "perfect love drives out fear" (1 Jn 4:18). In other words, if I really believe that God loves me, my husband, and my children, that knowledge will drive away my fear. Henri Nouwen writes in *Lifesigns* that "fear never gives birth to love" (p. 18). I need to remember that.

But fear is not my only enemy. One of the dark sides of my own independence is a sense that I am responsible for other people's problems. After all, they *need* me to do the job, if they want it done well, don't they?

When I believe that, I believe another lie. The truth is that our children's lives, "like ours, are shaped more by failure than by success, more by pain than by failure" (*Learning to Let Go,* Carol Kuykendall, Zondervan, 1985, p. 61). When I try to protect my children from the pain of failure, I risk depriving them of spiritual blessing.

"Consider it pure joy, my brothers," writes James, "whenever you face trials of many kinds, because you know that the testing of your faith develops perseverance. Perseverance must finish its work so that you may be mature and complete, not lacking anything" (Jas 1:2-4). "Suffering produces perseverance; perseverance, character; and character, hope" (Rom 5:3-4).

Malcolm Muggeridge, well-known English writer, wrote, "Contrary to what might be expected, I look back on experiences that at the time seemed especially desolating and painful with particular satisfaction. Indeed, everything I have learned, everything that has truly enhanced and enlightened my existence, has been through affliction and not through happiness. If it ever were to be possible to eliminate affliction from our earthly existence, the result would not be to make life delectable, but to make it too banal and trivial to be endurable" *(A Twentieth-Century Testimony,* Nelson, 1978). I am afraid that sometimes my efforts are aimed at eliminating affliction from Elisa and Dorie's lives, but I dare not deprive them of the hope, the growth or the maturity which come through suffering and pain. Instead, I must let them make their own choices, even when I think they may lead to suffering, and then try to be there when they need extra support to face the results.

But that is easier said than done. I am still left struggling with the gray areas. Carol Kuykendall suggests that when we face questions about how independent to let our children be, we should ask ourselves, "Whose problem is it?" Is it my problem or my child's? If it is his problem, I need to let him solve it and live with the consequences of his solution. If his behavior affects me, then we need to solve it together. If it is my problem, then I need to solve it myself.

I know of one mother who was almost standing on her head trying to get her first-grader out the door to school on time. After many mornings of fighting and frustration, the mother decided it was not her problem and that if her son was late to school, he would learn from the consequences. Needless to say, when Mother stopped taking responsibility for the problem, Son picked it up and got himself to school on time.

On the other hand, when our girls were young, I had a problem with the level of clutter in our playroom. The clutter didn't bother them, but it did bother me. So I said we had to keep the door shut. My problem. My solution. The only restriction I placed on the clutter was that I had to be able to freely open and close the door when I needed to get in and out of the room. If I couldn't do that, then it became a mutual problem because their behavior affected me. Most of the time it worked. I could get in and out. If not, they had to clear the clutter.

The older children get, of course, the higher the stakes. This is why most experts tell us to start the lessons of independence young. I wish I had started when the girls were younger. But the experts also tell us that it is never too late to begin!

My exaggerated sense of responsibility goes hand in hand with the other problem I have in letting my children go: I like to be needed. I like it when someone asks me for help, or, better yet, for advice! It boosts my self-esteem. But then when my children's needs and requests become demands, I become resentful and angry.

This is one of the threads of codependency. When a relationship becomes entrenched in a pattern of dependency, then the thread becomes a rope—and it can bind the relationship in painful and destructive ways. In an overly dependent relationship, one person feels unable to live, make decisions or make choices without the other's approval. The other person is so addicted to being needed that he cannot accept his own needs if they interfere with the needs of his "dependent other." He cannot say no to the other's requests, and his life revolves around keeping the other happy.

This is a very subtle and insidious phenomenon. It can happen in adult relationships. It can happen in parent-child relationships. Rather than binding our children to us, we need to be working ourselves out of a job, out of responsibility for their problems.

For some of us, this is a scary thing to do. We may have taught ourselves that our self-worth depends upon how much people—our children, our friends or our family—need us and how much we can help them. Carmen Berry, in *When Helping You Is Hurting Me,* calls this the "Messiah Trap." If we think that someone we know really cannot get along without our help, we may be playing God in that person's life. We may be doing good things for the wrong reasons. And we may be moving fast in exactly the opposite direction from where we want to go.

In my mind, the person who models the best parental position in this issue of independence versus dependence is God himself. "God gave all humans—His supreme creation—considerable freedom, and that includes the opportunity to goof up. . . . When Adam and Eve made the wrong choice, God allowed them to suffer the consequences. Although He did not approve of their disobedience, He loved them enough to let them make a decision and to live with the results. . . . God's love in the garden sets the example for all parents to follow: He allowed Adam and Eve the freedom to make the choice" (Foster Cline and Jim Fay, *Parenting with Love and Logic,* Nav-Press, 1990, pp. 26-27).

God does not err on the side of being overly protective. He allows us great freedom, great independence. He wants us to depend upon him in the sense that we trust him and have faith in his love for us. But he never takes away our freedom by making our choices for us.

If we follow God's example in loving our children into independence, then we may need to let our children live with the consequences of poor choices. Cline and Fay go on to say that "parents may refuse to allow their children to fail because they see such a response as uncaring. Thus they overcompensate with worry and hyper-concern. What these parents are doing, in reality, is meeting their own selfish needs. . . . Protection is not synonymous with caring, but both are part of love" (pp. 29-30).

Does this mean we feed and clothe our children and then send them out to face the world alone? Of course not. Again, God gives us an example. In his prayer at the end of his life, Moses described God "like an eagle that stirs up its nest and hovers over its young, that spreads its wings to catch them and carries them on its pinions" (Deut 32:11).

I was reading Deuteronomy one time when Dorie was in Middle School. She was at a point in life where a little more independence would have been appropriate. But neither Dorie nor I wanted to move in that direction. She was more than comfortable in the nest, and I was quite content to keep her there, under my wings. But when I read about the eagle in Moses' prayer, I could hardly wait for Dorie to get home from school.

"Dorie," I said, "I need to be more like an eagle. I need to push you out of the nest. I won't like it and you won't like it. But after I push, I'll swoop down and be there if you fall." We both liked that image, and we both agreed to try. This past Christmas, Dorie's last at home before college, she gave me a framed picture of an eagle, complete with the verse that had motivated us to take a necessary step toward her maturity.

My friends who have boys as well as girls tell me that parenting little boys is a different experience from parenting little girls. I wonder if learning independence isn't one area where the difference stands out. Sociologists and psychologists tell us that as little boys grow up, they are taught to become independent of their mothers ("be a man"). Little girls, on the other hand, are taught to become "just like mommy." Perhaps dependency issues look different, then, for parents and daughters than for parents and sons. Boys may have a harder time learning dependence, while girls may have a harder time learning independence.

I suspect, however, that these issues go far deeper than gender differences. In fact, I suspect this is one area where the influence of past generations is deeply felt. If my parents did not trust me and made me too dependent, then I may overcompensate by pushing my children out too fast. Or if my parents did not get involved enough in my life, then I may be tempted to overreact by clinging too tightly to my children.

Here is yet another area where we need to pray for grace to look at ourselves honestly and for wisdom to influence our children lovingly. May God give us love to hold our children closely and grace to let them go.

For Personal Reflection
1. In your most honest moments, do you sense that you push your children too quickly toward independence, hold them back and keep them too dependent, or have a good balance between dependence and independence?

If your children are old enough, ask them how they would answer this question for you.

2. Carmen Berry observes that people caught in the "Messiah Trap" often feel one of two things: "If I don't do it, it won't get done" or "Everyone else's needs take priority over mine." Are you inclined to have either of these feelings? When? What effect do these feelings have on your style of parenting?

Can you think of a time recently when you or your spouse may have "played God" in your child's life by getting overinvolved? How would you behave differently another time?

3. As you think of each of your children, what differences do you notice in their responses to being independent? What influences in their lives would account for these differences? What is the next step of growth toward independence that each child needs to take?

4. The following poem describes one person's view of "letting go." Write three or four more lines which describe your own view.

To "Let Go" Takes Love
To "let go" does not mean to stop caring,
  it means I can't do it for someone else.
To "let go" is not to cut myself off, it is
  the realization I can't control another.
To "let go" is not to enable, but to allow
  learning from natural consequences.
To "let go" is to admit powerlessness, which
  means the outcome is not in my hands.
To "let go" is not to try to change or blame
  another, it is to make the most of myself.
To "let go" is not to care for, but to care about.
To "let go" is not to fix, but to be supportive.
To "let go" is not to judge, but to allow another
  to be a human being.

To "let go" is not to be in the middle arranging all the
  outcomes but to allow others to affect their own destinies.
To "let go" is not to be protective, it is to
  permit another to face reality.
To "let go" is not to deny, but to accept.
To "let go" is not to nag, scold, or argue, but instead
  to search out my own shortcomings and to correct them.
To "let go" is not to adjust everything to my desires but to
  take each day as it comes, and to cherish myself in it.
To "let go" is not to criticize and regulate anybody
  but to try to become what I dream I can be.
To "let go" is to not regret the past, but to grow
  and to live for the future.
To "let go" is to fear less and to love more.

Author Unknown

For Group Discussion

1. Tell about one situation in your childhood which illustrates the amount of independence you experienced in your family.

2. In *Please Don't Say You Need Me* (Zondervan, 1989), Jan Silvious writes, "Pain is the purest motivator for change" (p. 33). When has one member of your family been painfully dependent on you, or painfully independent of you? What did you do with that pain? How could you use the pain as a motivation to make appropriate changes?

3. God describes himself as a mother eagle, pushing her young out of the nest. What animal picture would best describe the way you relate to your children?

4. If you had been God, would you have let Adam and Eve do what they wanted in the garden, even though it included disobedience? Why or why not?

Chapter 7
How Are We Different?
Let Me Count the Ways

I am a Winter, INFJ, Thyroid Type. Now you know all about me, right? Wrong. Now you know (if you are familiar with the same categories I am) what colors I like to wear, some of my temperament traits and what I like to eat. These categories are luxuries for those of us who like categories. They are not necessities, and they certainly are not all we need for healthy relationships. Thanks to our imaginative, creative God, categories do not tell all we need to know about another person.

One of the most wonderful things about being a parent is the privilege of watching a person *become*. There is no one else in the whole world, there never has been anyone else in the whole world, exactly like the child you are parenting. To say "God made you special" is an understatement. God made each one of us so special that sometimes we surprise even ourselves!

As we parent the children God has put in our charge, we do well to take notice of their unique characteristics. This means that we will have to set aside some of our own preferences and prejudices in order to observe and affirm theirs. It means, too, looking at each child with a mindset that asks, "What makes this person original, different from anyone else in the family and in the world?" In our own family, Bob and I have found at least three specific areas where acknowledging differences is especially helpful.

One of the first areas of differences that surfaced as our children began to socialize with others was the difference between those who prefer interaction with people over time to be alone. Some children (and adults) are refreshed and energized by being with people. Others are emotionally and physically drained by social interaction. This phenomenon has nothing to do with how much love a person has for other people. It does not always have to do with how much a person wants to be with other people. It has to do, most of all, with where a person finds refreshment and restoration. An extroverted person finds refreshment by going out and interacting with others. An introverted person finds refreshment by being alone for a while.

I am an introvert. Some time ago I talked with Susan, a very extroverted friend. "When you are feeling low," I asked her, "when you feel a little sad, what do you do to help yourself feel better?" "Well," she answered in her southern drawl, "I do feel that way sometimes on Sunday afternoons when I'm home all alone. Then I just make sure I go to church that night. Church always lifts my spirits." I could hardly believe my ears! That is one of the last things I would think of doing if I was feeling low! I love God's people. I go to church regularly. I have been a leader in most of the churches I have attended. But when I come home from church on Sunday, I am exhausted. Not because I don't love God or want to go to church. But because three or four hours of interaction with other people wears me out. I need to be alone to recuperate.

A year or two after this conversation, I had occasion to visit Susan in the hospital. As I walked to her room, way at the end of the hall, I thought to myself, "How nice. Susan has a quiet room." But by the time I knocked on her door, I had remembered that a room at the end of a long hall might not be so nice for Susan. Sure enough. She was feeling pretty well. "But this room," she said. "I have to walk all the way down the hall to the nurses' station to find anyone to talk to!"

Do you think that Susan is a "better" person because she is energized by going to church? Or do you think that I am a "better" person because I make good use of peace and quiet? Quite frankly, I don't think God minds what our preferences are in this area. He cares about each of us, but does he want me to become an extrovert or Susan an introvert? Nothing in Scripture tells me so.

It is critical for parents to notice and accept their children's differences in this area. This may be especially difficult (and important) if your child is an introvert. Generally speaking, children love to play together. Even introvert children like to be with their friends. But their need for social interaction may be more limited than most people realize. When our girls (both introverts) were young, I couldn't count the number of times I heard, "Oh, bring your children! There will be other kids there, and I'm just sure they'd love to play together!" Yes, my children loved to play with other children, but usually not as often or as long as my extrovert friends might think. It takes some willingness to be different, to admit that there are times when your child would rather be alone than out playing with friends.

Statistically, seventy-five per cent of all people are extroverts, twenty-five per cent introverts. That means that three-fourths of the population prefers a lifestyle which one-fourth finds difficult to maintain. I assume that God intended for there to be more extroverts than introverts. (Otherwise, Christian community would be hard indeed!) But I am also convinced that God uses his quiet, reflective introverts, just as he uses outgoing, social extroverts. It would be a violation of his creative variety if we tried to force our introvert children into extrovert molds.

Another difference which we have found very helpful to observe in our family is the difference in the ways we are each motivated to action. Persons who are "internally" motivated look within to determine what they really want to do. Persons who are "externally" motivated get motivation from other people, from rewards, or from some source outside of themselves. Again, there are advantages and disadvantages to both ways of being. The internally motivated person has the obvious advantage of not being dependent upon other people in order to get going. The externally motivated person has the advantage of using rewards as tools, as well as the advantage of being more open to the influence and help of others.

Most children start out externally motivated. Maturity includes learning to motivate yourself to do a job that has to be done. But even adults have a general "bent" toward internal or external motivation. I have a friend who is very mature and very responsible. But she finds that she still does well to build some external motivation into her life when she faces a particularly unpleasant task. So, she promises herself rewards when the job is done, she sets the kitchen timer to be sure she sticks to the task a certain length of time, and she gives herself other incentives in order to accomplish what she wants to do.

Children, of course, do not have the maturity to set up such systems for themselves. That is why when Elisa began piano lessons, I made a "Coupon Book" of prizes she could earn by practicing a given amount of time. She was at the age when every little girl wants her own horse, so one of the prizes was a horse—but unfortunately, the page that offered horses was always over-written with "OUT OF STOCK"! Pages which were usually in stock included games, stuffed animals, a trip to Showbiz Pizza, and other fabulous prizes! Elisa used the Coupon Book to motivate herself to practice the piano.

Wanting to be a "fair" parent, I offered Dorie a reward for practicing the piano, also. After a certain number of hours, I said, I would take her to buy a beautiful beige dress we had seen at a local store.

The problem was that rewards have never worked with Dorie. She has a strong bent to be internally motivated, so the opportunity to gain a reward meant very little to her. Once again, we learned that life is not always fair. Elisa earned many prizes for practicing. Dorie practiced on her own (and got the dress for "free").

Our job as parents is not to make one child like the other (or like us), but to notice and respect their differences and to help them grow in the ways that fit them best. Elisa has now learned to practice on her own, without rewards from me. In fact, she has learned to reward herself in many areas of life, exhibiting initiative and responsibility which many adults would envy. Dorie still enjoys her internal motivation, works hard at motivating herself, and is learning how to handle situations where her internal motivation is not as strong as she would like. They are both moving toward maturity in their own unique ways.

Finally, as I think of differences among children, I think of differing gifts and talents. Dorie and Elisa were still preschoolers when Dr. James Dobson wrote *Hide or Seek*. In it, he said, "The current epidemic of self-doubt has resulted from a totally unjust and unnecessary system of evaluating human worth, now prevalent in our society. Not everyone is seen as worthy; not everyone is accepted. Instead, we reserve praise and admiration for a select few who have been blessed from birth with the characteristics we value most highly" (*Hide or Seek*, Revell, 1974, p. 12).

Dobson goes on to identify the two most common standards for evaluating personal worth in our society: beauty and intelligence. I would add money, social ease, athletic ability, and, for some Christians, even spirituality. How do we help a child who may not score a "10" in all these areas? We help him by readjusting our values so that who he is becomes valuable.

If there is one special gift that a mother and father can give to every child, it is this: letting the child know that he or she is uniquely gifted to do something very well, thereby helping the child look for the special contribution he or she can make to other people and to the kingdom of God.

I have learned much from Dr. Dobson, as well as from other authors who have written about the importance of helping each child develop a solid base of appropriate self-esteem. But I find this yet another road in the parenting experience which is hard to walk.

Almost more than anything else, I want my children to know that they are loved and valued for who they are and not for who someone else wishes they were. My attempts at convincing them of this are hampered on one side by those who say "You can do anything you set your mind to do. The world is out there waiting for you!" That is an unrealistic lie. On the other hand, there are those who imply that if I praise or affirm my children too much, I run the risk of spoiling them and teaching selfishness and pride.

And there is also the built-in human resistance to accepting love and affirmation. One of the greatest spiritual tragedies of mankind is that we do not easily accept the love of God. Likewise, it is sometimes hard for me to accept my husband's love, and it is sometimes hard for our children to accept our love and affirmation. It is as though we have holes in our "love buckets"—as love is poured into them, it seems to leak out.

And so, once again we who are parents need to pray with great urgency. We need to pray that our children will learn to value the gifts God has given them, that they will learn to accept our affirmation of those gifts, and that they will learn to receive our love and the love of God the Father for them.

Sometimes all we can do is pray. But often God want us to do more than pray. We need to regularly remind our children of areas where they have shown growth and success. We need to praise their efforts, with appropriate affirmation. We also need to share our own struggles and weaknesses with them, so that they do not feel alone in the process of growing.

At one particularly low point in Dorie's life we had a WE-LOVE-YOU-DORIE Dinner, complete with cake and gifts.

At another time, when Elisa was quite young and going through a rough time, we started a "Compliment Book" which hung by a string on her bedpost for about a year. I tried to remember to write down compliments for her, sometimes every day, sometimes once a week. Other members of the family, as well as an adult friend or two, added their compliments.

Last spring we all had a good laugh as we read through the Compliment Book, having forgotten about it for several years. The compliments ranged from corny ("Breakfast"—a poem—"Elisa ate her eggs, Elisa ate her toast. Elisa ate her bacon, Mom thinks that's the most!") to serious ("I love you and admire you. You've done a super job studying spelling. I appreciate your telling me what you are thinking, whether it's happy or sad. Last night was sad, remember? And you did a great job on Sunday practicing a hard piece on the piano.") The book will be a treasure to cherish for a long time.

In many ways the Bible is God's Compliment Book to us. In it he tells us that he loves us. He reminds us that he is interested in us, that he forgives us, and that he has given us talents and abilities which he enjoys watching us use. His acceptance, love and gifts look different to each of us. The more we appreciate these differences, the more we stand in awe of God's unparalleled creativity and his unique love for what he has created.

For Personal Reflection
1. Answer the following questions about each of your children (if they are old enough, ask them for their help!).
(1) Do you sense that _____ is more of an extrovert or introvert? Is _____ refreshed by being with people or by being alone? What is the best thing you can do to help this child in making good use of this preference?

(2) Is _____ more apt to be motivated by his or her internal desires or by external rewards, pressures or suggestions? What evidence do you have for this? How can you help this child be motivated?

(3) List the personality traits, temperament qualities, and/or talents of _____. What opportunities does this child have to express these? What other opportunities could you facilitate?

2. Looking over your answers to the questions above, in what ways are you like each child? In what ways are you different? Do your similarities and differences enhance or hinder your parenting ability?

3. In what ways is your spouse like or unlike each child? Do you sense that these similarities and differences help or hinder him/her as a parent?

4. Meditate on Psalm 139:13-16. What are some of the things about your own "inmost being" that you like most? Identify some of the threads (characteristics, gifts and so on) that are "woven together" in you. What is one unique gift or quality which you have that you like to share with other people?

For Group Discussion
1. What things do other people do for you which help you embrace and enjoy your own uniqueness?

What things do you try to do for your children to help them enjoy their uniqueness?

2. What differences in people are most difficult for you to accept: introvert/extrovert differences? differences in motivation? differences in gifts? other differences? What reasons can you give for your difficulty in accepting these differences? How does this affect your relationship with your children?

3. Paul wrote to the Corinthians that each person has some "manifestation of the Spirit." Read 1 Corinthians 12:7-11 to see examples of these manifestations. List all the members of your family. What manifestations of the Spirit does each person have?

4. What effect do you think television and movies have on children's ability to accept their uniqueness? on their self-esteem?

5. Share some creative things you do in your family to help your family members affirm and enjoy each other's differences.

Chapter 8
What Do We Do about Sibling Rivalry?

It is a comfort to me that sibling rivalry does not surprise God.

The first relationship which was broken as a result of sin was the relationship between God and man. (Adam hid from God, Gen 3:10.) The second relationship damaged by sin was the husband-wife relationship. (Adam blamed Eve, Gen 3:12.) The third relationship hurt by sin was the sibling relationship between Cain and Abel (Gen 4:1-12). Cain was the first-born, a farmer; Abel was his younger brother, a shepherd. When it came time for the brothers to offer sacrifices to God, Cain brought "fruits of the soil," and Abel brought the "first-born of his flock." God approved of Abel's offering. He did not approve of Cain's.

Biblical scholars have offered many reasons why Abel's sacrifice was acceptable and Cain's was not. Did it have to do with the attitude of each brother? Or did it reflect God's demand for a blood sacrifice, later fulfilled in Jesus? We can only guess. The thing we can say for certain is that Scripture itself does not answer the question.

Perhaps in the long run a non-answer is the most satisfying answer. Most of life's difficult questions do not have adequate answers. Why is my brother so smart, when I can barely get B's? Why is my sister so pretty, or popular or thin, when I am so ugly, lonely or fat? Anyone who has grown up with brothers or sisters can tell you a hundred reasons why life is not fair. As adults, most of us are reconciled to this lack of equality. But children, the champions of fairness, are not.

At first, life's injustices between our daughters could be solved relatively easily. One divided the cookie and the other got to choose first. But as our girls grew older, sibling rivalry became more and more difficult. And nothing, absolutely nothing, tears at my heartstrings more than sibling rivalry.

One day, after a particularly intense squabble, I retreated to the living room, flopped down in despair and cried out, "Lord, what am I supposed to do?" For lack of any better idea, I picked up a magazine from the coffee table to read while I cooled off. I flipped it open to an article by a well-known parenting expert. The article included a picture of this man at one of his large teaching sessions. The caption under the picture read, "Concerning sibling rivalry: There is little you can do. Just be sure there is no blood." Thank you, Lord, for that reminder. I am not alone.

There is, in fact, little we can do to avoid all sibling rivalry. When Elisa was born, the pediatrician reminded me that Dorie might have some of the feelings I would have if Bob brought home a second wife. Similarly, Elisa would have to deal with the potential resentment of arriving after the party had already started. The addition of a third or fourth child would have brought another set of built-in jealousies. On top of these birth-order "handicaps" come life's inequalities of beauty, intelligence, popularity, even spirituality. What's a parent to do?

We cannot make life fair. In fact, part of maturity is learning that life is not always fair. But we can foster a family environment where our children experience love even when life is not fair.

One of the first things we can do to foster this environment is to *acknowledge that each of our children was born into a different family.* When Dorie was born, we became a family of three. When Elisa was born, we were already a family, but now we became a family of four. In other words, Dorie and Elisa were born into "different" families. Psychologists and sociologists have identified some of the major effects differences in birth order produce in children. Dr. Kevin Leman wrote *The Birth Order Book,* which defines many common characteristics of first-born children, second-born, and on down the line.

This does not mean that any of our children will fit a birth-order mold, but it does remind us that we must never expect our children to be alike in every way, and it reassures us that no matter what we do, there will be some birth-order phenomenon which will influence our children whether we like it or not. First-born children often struggle with perfectionism. Last-born children may become family clowns. Being a perfectionist or being a clown both have potential for good and potential for danger. What we do with our own birth-order characteristics and how we help our children manage theirs is what makes the difference.

Another thing we can do, besides recognizing birth-order differences, is to *avoid playing favorites.* But all good parents know that. So why do we forget so easily? Why did Isaac and Rebekah play favorites? (See Gen 25 and 27.) Even if we are careful not to make comparisons, sometimes our friends do it for us. How can we respond to this manifestation of life's unfairness?

We can make every effort to build up each child in light of his or her particular gifts and talents. We can give honest compliments. ("You certainly bring laughter into our family!" "You are the most organized child I know.") In our house, we learned the hard way to avoid hand-me-down clothes whenever possible because they are not worth the money they save when the uniqueness of a child is sacrificed. We have learned not to assume preferences—in food, amusements, school activities, clothes, restaurants, whatever. And we are learning that following in a sibling's footsteps is not necessarily a virtue.

A third way we can deal with the tensions of siblings is to *spend time alone with each child.* Not because we owe each child equal time, but because we love each child individually. We can make sure each child has opportunities to express himself or herself independently of the brothers and sisters.

Elisa and I had a wonderful time one day when her school was off for the day and Dorie's was not. Elisa slept in, and I covered up all the clocks in the house. Later, I left my watch at home when we went to breakfast, lunch, shopping, the library and bowling without letting ourselves see a clock! That day will be a "timeless" memory for Elisa and me. We both loved it! On the other hand, Dorie and I have spent days doing things together which would utterly bore Elisa. What a joy for me to have two very different daughters to take away for the day!

The parable of the prodigal son is sometimes called the parable of the prodigal brother because of the older brother's negative response to his sibling's welcome home (Lk 15:28-30). I agree that the older brother could (and should) have been much more merciful and forgiving in his attitude. But I have seen grown men and women cry like little children because they were neglected by their parents. The older brother needed to take responsibility for his own sinful pride, but there is a warning here to us as parents. There will always be times when one child needs to take precedence over another, but if this becomes a pattern of neglect, we will be introducing deep pain into our children's lives. It is a big, almost impossible, job to be a responsible, fair parent to all our children. We need God's help to do that.

A final word about sibling rivalry. I have had to learn the hard way that one of the worst things to do with older siblings is to interfere, to try to make life fair (from your point of view). It is sobering to think of what happened when Laban interfered in the lives of his daughters Leah and Rachel (Gen 29:16—30:24). By deceiving Jacob so that he married Leah instead of Rachel, Laban may not have done Leah a great service. Evidence is that instead of resolving their differences, these sisters suffered from sibling rivalry for the rest of their lives. There are times when the best thing we can do for our children is to stay out of their lives, especially out of their sibling rivalries.

I am convinced, however, that no parent can avoid all forms of sibling rivalry. There is, in fact, some good in it.

Sibling rivalry may actually help children grow spiritually and socially. Proverbs 27:17 could have been written specifically for siblings: "As iron sharpens iron, so one [brother or sister] sharpens another." Brothers and sisters, that is, help each other so that each becomes a better person.

There are painful parts of growing up. There are sharp edges to be smoothed out. There are sinful tendencies that need to be frequently addressed. What better place for this to happen than in the family, where love usually predominates. Who is better equipped to help us with this growth process than mother, father, sister or brother? It may be painful, but it is part of God's plan, and it is another reason why life in the family is good.

For Personal Reflection
1. List five personality traits and five talents of each of your children.

What observations can you make from these lists? Does one child have more "visible" strengths than the others? What can you do to encourage a less visible child?

2. Is one child more like you than the others? In what ways? What effect does it have on you to share some of the same strengths and weaknesses with your child?

3. Are you a first-born, second-born or third-born child? How does this influence your parenting style?

4. What do you think God wants you to do in the coming weeks to build up each one of your children?

For Group Discussion
1. What are your best childhood memories of times spent with

your own brothers and sisters?

What was the most difficult aspect of your relationship with your siblings?

2. Read the account of Isaac's family in Genesis 27:1-40. What mistakes did Isaac and Rebekah make? Why do you think they might have made these mistakes? When are you most tempted to show favoritism in your own family?

3. In what ways do your own children reflect typical birth-order patterns? In what ways are they different from the patterns? How do you respond to birth-order differences in your family? What do you do to help each child feel special?

4. Read about Leah and Rachel in Genesis 29:14—30:24. What was the result of Laban's interference? Do you think he was right to interfere? Why or why not? Did your parents ever interfere in your relationship with your siblings? What effect did that have?

5. What is one specific way people can pray for you in regard to the issues of sibling rivalry in your own family?

Pray for one another.

Chapter 9
What Do I Do with My Anger?
Good and Bad Anger

Christopher screamed in terror. Kathleen wakened with a start, her heart beating fast. She jumped out of bed and raced into her son's room just as he screamed again. Christopher was not asleep. It was not a dream. The monster was about to attack.

But as his mother ran into his room, she flipped on the light, and the monster was gone.

"Christopher, Christopher, what's wrong?"

"Oh, Mommy! There was a big monster over there in the corner. I know there was. Oh, Mommy! Don't leave me!"

Kathleen looked in the corner. Of course, no monster lurked there behind the wastebasket. But she knew her son had seen something. He was not given to hysterics, and he did not lie. She turned out the light. The monster re-appeared!

"Oh, look, Christopher! The monster is only the shadow of the trash coming out of your wastebasket. See, the night light makes a shadow on the wall from all this paper you threw out."

That night a monster had terrified Christopher. But it could have been worse. Even worse than having a monster attack you is feeling as if there is a monster inside of you, or feeling as if you are a monster yourself. I want to speak the language of love to my children, but there have been times when I have been so angry that I have, indeed, felt like a monster. Like a lion-monster, to be exact. The lion is raging inside me, and yet, at the same time, I feel as if I am the lion, raging in a cage I cannot leave.

Anger is like that, consuming us from within and ensnaring us from without. I know lots of angry people, but I do not know anyone who *likes* to be angry. I do not know anyone who likes to be a monster, or who likes to be trapped inside the cage of anger.

But anger is a fact of life. Amazingly, it is not only a fact of human life, but also a fact of divine life. God himself gets angry. So angry that the Old Testament writers describe his anger as fierce, hot, burning, great, furious, jealous and fiery. There have been moments in my parenting experience when I have felt furious, fierce anger.

And I feel very guilty about that anger. Some of the guilt I feel is accurate—real guilt because I have sinned in my anger. Unlike God, my anger is not always righteous. Unlike God, I do not always do the right thing with my anger.

But before we look at the negative side of anger, we must come to terms with the phenomenon of anger itself.

Anger is not inherently bad. It is almost always unpleasant, but not always sinful. In fact, of all the references to anger in the Bible, the overwhelming majority refer to the anger of God. The historical books of the Old Testament as well as the books of prophecy describe God's anger in such strong terms that I would be embarrassed to have someone describe me that way.

"Alice unleashed her anger. It consumed Dorie and Elisa like stubble. . . . She made them look absolutely dreadful and horrible. . . . She even trampled them to the ground. She got their blood on her own clothes." Sounds gruesome, doesn't it? But see Exodus 15:7; 2 Chronicles 29:8; and Isaiah 63:3 for similar descriptions of God's anger toward his people.

Does this description of God give me license for child abuse? Not at all. *God's anger is always good anger.* Our anger is often self-seeking, sinful anger. We need to learn from Scripture how we can tell the difference between good anger and bad anger, but first we need to be sure we do not throw out the baby with the bath water. If I assume that every flash of anger I feel is sinful, I may miss the good anger. If I say that anger is always sin, as some Christians do, I may miss the benefits of following in God's footsteps—even when he is angry.

In fact, if I deny my own anger, I may miss something good that God wants to do with my anger. Ezekiel said that he went to the exiles in Tel Abib in bitterness and in anger, with the "strong hand of the LORD" upon him (Ezek 3:14). Is it possible to be filled with the Holy Spirit and be angry at the same time? Apparently so. I need to remember that.

But I also need to remember that my own anger is often permeated with my own sinfulness. I have no illusions about the dark side of my anger. I have slammed doors, shouted criticisms, even thrown a cup of cranberry juice across the kitchen. (It was a plastic cup, and I did aim it in the direction of the sink, but I still do not recommend that way of expressing anger!) Those were times when my anger was not good. It was sin.

How, then, can we tell the difference? How do we know what is good anger and what is sinful anger?

Good anger has four characteristics: it is *slow in coming,* it is *restrained in expression,* it is *temporary in extent,* and it is *forgiving.* These are all characteristics of God's anger, and if we find that our own anger does not have these characteristics, we should look carefully to see if pride, selfishness or some other sin is influencing our angry responses.

First of all, good anger is slow anger. Rage, in contrast, feels more like flood waters racing through my body and out my mouth. Or, as Maggie Scarf wrote in the *New York Times Magazine,* "Getting angry can sometimes be like leaping into a wonderfully responsive sports car, gunning the motor, taking off at high speed and then discovering the brakes are out of order." In contrast, God's anger is slow in coming. "You, O LORD, are a compassionate and gracious God, slow to anger, abounding in love and faithfulness" (Ps 86:15). Perhaps the most appropriate response we can have when we first feel anger is to tell ourselves to "Slow Down!"

Good anger is also restrained anger. "He was merciful; he forgave their iniquities and did not destroy them. Time after time he restrained his anger and did not stir up his full wrath" (Ps 78:38). "A fool gives full vent to his anger, but a wise man keeps himself under control" (Prov 29:11). In other words, I am stronger than the monster. I do not have to give him free reign. I can keep him in his place, behind the wastebasket.

Good anger does not last very long. "For his [God's] anger lasts only a moment, but his favor lasts a lifetime" (Ps 30:5). "He [God] will not always accuse, nor will he harbor his anger forever" (Ps 103:9). " 'In a surge of anger I hid my face from you for a moment, but with everlasting kindness I will have compassion on you,' says the LORD your Redeemer" (Is 54:8). Perhaps this is why we are told not to go to bed angry (see Eph 4:26). If we can't get rid of our anger before sundown, perhaps it is not good anger.

A few days ago, Dorie and Elisa had a huge fight shortly after dinner. Tempers flared. Angry words shot back and forth across the room. The immediate cause of the fight was incidental (I don't even remember it). Both girls knew they were venting angry feelings that had been festering for months. Perhaps some "good anger" along the way would have served them better, but it was too late for that now.

I was upstairs washing the kitchen floor. As I heard the anger come up the steps, I found myself tempted to panic, condemn or join in and mediate. But for once I did it right. I stayed out. As I pushed the mop back and forth across the floor, I prayed, "Lord, just don't let the sun go down on their wrath." (I always revert to King James English when I'm upset!) "Just don't let the sun go down. . . ." Mop. Mop. Fight. Fight. Finally things subsided into tears and angry footsteps.

A little while later, Elisa came and said she was ready to talk it out. Thank you, Lord. Thank you, Elisa. Dorie said she was willing to talk. Thank you, Dorie. Both girls sat down and talked through their angry feelings. God turned bad anger into good anger. The sun did not go down on their wrath.

And, finally, good anger is forgiving anger. This may be the key to the difference between sinful anger and God's anger. "The LORD is slow to anger, abounding in love and forgiving sin and rebellion" (Num 14:18). "You are a forgiving God, gracious and compassionate, slow to anger and abounding in love. Therefore you did not desert them" (Neh 9:17). Forgiveness does not mean ignoring the hurt or the anger. It means restoring the relationship. It means saying, either in words or in actions, "I want to return to the loving, supportive parent-child relationship we had before we got angry." It means willfully and consciously setting aside our angry feelings.

That may take time. Sometimes we need to feel our hurt or process our anger. If we deny our anger because it embarrasses us or because we are too afraid of its potential for sin, then we cannot forgive. Forgiveness means admitting that the relationship has been broken, and then offering restoration.

I believe that forgiveness, compassion and mercy most often need to originate with the parent. We love because God, our Father, loved us first (1 Jn 4:19). When it is time to set our anger aside, more often than not the parent needs to take the first step. There are exceptions, of course, but sulking, bitterness, malice and constant quarreling are not options for those of us who want to parent our children as God parents us.

Fortunately, God has promised that he will *always* help us overcome our predisposition to sin, whether the sin is in withholding forgiveness or in some other manifestation of bad anger. God's Word promises that "no temptation has seized you except what is common to man. And God is faithful; he will not let you be tempted beyond what you can bear. But when you are tempted, he will also provide a way out so that you can stand up under it" (1 Cor 10:13).

In other words, there is *always* a way out of bad anger. There is no anger that can overwhelm us forever. In spite of the fact that I sometimes feel like a caged, roaring lion, I am not, in truth, caged. God will provide a way to escape. In the next chapter we will look at some of the ways God helps us in our anger, at some of the reasons for anger and at some ways we can make sure our anger stays "good anger."

For Personal Reflection

1. What do you do when you get angry? What do you say? What do you look like? Where do you go?

2. Circle the word which best describes how you feel about your own anger.

embarrassed   afraid   comfortable   unconscious guilty　　　　　confused　　　　　secure　　　　　ashamed

3. Think about the last time you were really angry with your children. Comment on the following questions:
How fast did you react in anger?

How did you express your anger?

How long did your anger last?

Did you resolve your anger? If so, how?

If you could re-enact this encounter with anger, what would you do differently?

4. Have you ever experienced God's anger? If so, what was that like for you? How do you think God expresses his anger today?

For Group Discussion

1. 1 Kings 14:22 reads, "[The people of] Judah did evil in the eyes of the LORD. By the sins they committed they stirred up his jealous anger more than their fathers had done." Why do you think God's anger is called "jealous"?

What things do you think people do today that stir up God's jealous anger?

What things do your children do that make you angry?

2. Proverbs 30:33 provides an interesting commentary on anger: "For as churning the milk produces butter, and as twisting the nose produces blood, so stirring up anger produces strife." What is the difference between being angry about something and "stirring up anger"? When are you most prone to stir up anger?

3. Which of the four characteristics of good anger is the most difficult for you? What practical steps could you take to help your anger be better anger?

4. "I will praise you, O LORD. Although you were angry with me, your anger has turned away and you have comforted me" (Is 12:1). What brings you comfort after you have been angry?

What brings your children comfort after anger? (If they are old enough, ask them.) Compare answers to see whether the group can identify some elements common to all children.

Chapter 10
What Do I Do with My Anger?
Looking for the Roots

When Kathleen turned on the light in Christopher's room, the monster created by the shadow of his wastebasket disappeared. In a similar way we can diffuse anger by shedding light on why we are angry and on what God thinks of our anger.

One day in particular comes to mind. It had been a bad day for me. Not a terrible day, just a bad day. Not a day of struggling with mountains of problems but of struggling with the grains of sand in my shoe.

One of the irritating grains was listening to my children complain about life and squabble with each other. By the time I was ready to go to bed, my emotional feet hurt. They were getting raw from the irritations.

My friends know that I am not an evening person. Don't even dial my phone number after 9:00! On the evening of this particular day, I was in the kitchen shortly after nine. As I lifted a full gallon of milk from the refrigerator shelf, someone started in with complaining again. The complaints, though minor, were the last straw for me. I turned around and said in a less-than-patient voice, "Would you please be quiet!" At the same time, I slammed the unopened gallon of milk on the kitchen counter. The plastic bottle did not just spill— it split right down the middle. My daughter and the dog immediately fled. I stood there, all alone, in my bathrobe, watching a gallon of milk run all over the counter, onto the floor and under the stove.

The lion-monster in me began to rage. Why did I have to listen to all those complaints? Why did my children have to fight? Why was our family so irritable? The lion roared on and on. Then I told him to "shut up!" As I picked up the towel and began to clean up the milk, I said to myself, "I will never tell anyone about this!"

I did go in and talk with my daughter, and we found a measure of peace before we went to bed. But when I woke up the next morning, I felt sad, bruised and guilty. I had failed.

Instead of bearing the fruits of the Spirit (peace, patience, self-control), I had given in to the acts of the sinful nature (discord, selfishness, fits of rage—Gal 5:19-21). And I felt confused. "God," I prayed, "give me wisdom to be the kind of mother you want me to be." With that request in mind, I sat down for my daily devotional time.

Setting aside my normal reading schedule, I decided to look at the book of James because I knew he talked about wisdom, and I was sure God wanted to reassure me. He did, but not in the way I expected. I read James 1:5: "If any of you lacks wisdom (that's me), he should ask God (I already had), who gives generously to all (that's good, I need it) *without finding fault. . . .*" I stopped there. "Without finding fault." That was the reassurance I needed to hear. God would not hold my failure with anger against me. His forgiving grace was a light on my monster that diffused its power.

God would forgive me. Yes, he would give me wisdom, but, today, right now, he would forgive me. What a gift. I could go on being a mother.

God's grace is, without a doubt, the most important source of light we can shed on our anger. Without his grace, I do not know how I could live with this powerful, sometimes frightening, emotion. But because of his grace, I can not only live with anger but sometimes even benefit from it.

Without a doubt, the greatest benefit of anger in my life is that it is a very important source of very important information. Anger is one of the first ways I notice that there is something wrong with a relationship. Perhaps I am too dependent, or perhaps I am just the opposite, too giving. Perhaps because of the relationship I am ignoring an important emotional issue in my own life. In the same way that physical pain often causes me to address illness or a physical problem, so my anger may cause me to look at an emotional need I have ignored.

Or perhaps my anger forces me to accept a reality about myself or the other person which I would prefer not to believe.

After God's grace had quieted my soul, I was able to look at the anger behind the spilled milk and see what it was saying to me. I was operating under the illusion that I was responsible for solving my children's problems. Their pain was my pain. And that made me angry. I had enough problems of my own! Their complaints played right into my illusion. They were not really saying this, but what I heard was, "Please fix my life."

My anger motivated me to examine that illusion and to pull back. My anger also made me address the illusion that my children could never get along in life without my advice and help. (They need to learn to be responsible for their own problems and anger.) Anger is good when it causes us to face reality and truth.

Norman Rohrer and S. Philip Sutherland develop this idea more fully in *Facing Anger* (Augsburg, 1981). They contend that we often hide behind anger because we want to believe we are powerful, self-sufficient, important and perfect, when, in fact, none of us is like that all of the time.

We need to feel *powerful.* I feel powerless, for example, when I cannot adequately help my children. The parent of a baby often feels powerless when the baby cries incessantly. The parent of a school-age child may feel powerless to motivate the child to do his homework. Often this sense of powerlessness leads to anger.

Likewise, most of us like to be independent and *self-sufficient.* We like to be able to "do it ourselves." But as parents, we often find ourselves in places where we are needy and find it difficult to cope. Our response to our own neediness? Often anger.

Or, consider that we like to be *important.* Importance comes when we are valued, especially when our feelings are valued. But what child can express adequate appreciation to the parent? And sometimes we do not even appropriately value ourselves. When we continually place our own feelings and desires at the bottom of the list, we will probably find ourselves angry.

And, finally, we would all like to be *perfect,* or at least look perfect. I would like to be perfectly patient, perfectly organized and perfectly calm. Children have a way of destroying such illusions. When my illusion of perfection is uncovered, I am tempted to be angry. Failure, then, often makes me mad.

It is sometimes helpful, therefore, to look at anger as a secondary emotion that we use to hide an illusion or expectation we have about ourselves. We may choose to be angry instead of admitting that we are weak, inadequate, less than important, or imperfect. We do not always do this on a conscious level. But if we listen, the monster of anger may actually be trying to tell us the truth.

What can we as parents do, then, with our anger?

We can take heart that anger is a divine as well as human emotion. We can receive comfort through God's forgiveness. And we can do our best to keep our anger from becoming rage, bitterness or malice (Eph 4:31).

One way to do this is to diffuse the anger by looking for an illusion it might be covering. We can ask ourselves, are we wishing we were more powerful in the relationship? Is that a legitimate wish or is it an illusion? Are we wishing we were less needy, more important, more perfect? Sometimes changes can be made which will correct an imbalance in the relationship. But sometimes we just have to live with the reality that we are not all we want to be.

It is of utmost importance that we as parents come to grips with this issue of anger—important not only for our own emotional and spiritual health, but also for that of our children.

When I taught a high-school Sunday-school class on conflict, a question came up about what frustrated the students most in their life at home. They told me that it was when their parents were angry and would not admit it. (They all came from Christian homes.)

Or I think of the thirty-year-old woman I met whose mother was an alcoholic. As a child, Carol remembers seeing her mother get angry. "Are you mad, Mommy?" she would ask. "NO! I AM NOT MAD!" her mother would shout. Small wonder that as an adult, Carol had trouble dealing with her own anger.

So what if we do admit our anger and look closely at its causes? Will this make anger pleasant? Not at all. But neither is surgery, a penicillin shot, discipline or any other painful experience which corrects something that has gone wrong. Personally, I hate anger, but I could not live without it. I have to work hard at finding acceptable ways to deal with it, express it and use it, but I still need anger. Anger, at least this side of heaven, is a necessary part of life.

For Personal Reflection

1. What illusion do you have about yourself which sometimes leads you to anger? Do you wish you were more powerful, more self-sufficient, more important, perfect? Or is there another illusion you wish to preserve?

2. Toward which family member do you tend to feel the most anger? Why?

With which family member do you tend to express the most anger? Why?

With which family member do you tend to express the least anger? Why?

3. List five things you have done or could do to make sure that in your anger you "do not sin" (Eph 4:26).
(1)

(2)

(3)

(4)

(5)

4. Read Psalm 4:4. When is silence the most appropriate response to your own anger? When is it better to express it? In what ways do you think God wants you to "search your heart" when you are angry?

For Group Discussion

Consider the following quotations from *Facing Anger:*
1. "To avoid feelings of weakness, they call on anger to give them a sense of strength" (p. 12). When have you seen this happen in your own life?

2. "Anger is not an automatic reflex that involuntarily erupts following a provocation. Angry people *choose* it to prevent a loss of self-esteem. It's a hedge against humiliation" (p. 15). Can you think of a situation where you have seen anger used in this way? What was the result?

3. "Anger is largely the result of unrealistic expectations. People who have realistic expectations about themselves and other people experience much less anger" (p. 31). Do you agree with this? How does being a Christian influence your expectations of yourself and of others? of your family?

4. "Importance comes from having our emotions acknowledged. . . . Being understood is more affirming than being praised. . . . When people understand my desires and also my fears of not getting my desires, then I feel understood" (p. 67). Would you rather be praised or "understood"?

Describe a time recently when you felt misunderstood by someone in your family. What happened?

When are your children most apt to feel misunderstood?

5. "To seek status is to be perpetually angry" (p. 74). Is anyone in your family "seeking status" within the family? in some other area of life? What can you do to help that person?

6. "Anger is our companion throughout life. God built it into the soul as a primary motivator for acceptance of reality, for growth, and for strength" (p. 127). In what ways are you thankful for your own anger? For your spouse's anger? For your children's anger?

Chapter 11
What about Spiritual Life in the Family?

Pregnancy was a hard time for us. Unlike the textbook predictions, I was out of commission not just for three months, but for virtually the entire, *long,* nine-month period.

The first time around, Bob had to adjust to marriage to a "different woman." The second time around, he often had to fulfill the role of both mother and father for Dorie. Labor and delivery were relatively long and difficult. Then when we finally got our baby daughters home and settled into the family, we realized we were less than half-done. Jesus said that they each had to be "born again"!

Unlike the first birth, which is identified by very graphic physical changes and attended by experts in medical care, the second birth is spiritual, not as obvious, slower and often accomplished in private. And yet this second birth is just as important as the first. We parents, furthermore, are often called upon to be the "experts" in attendance.

No matter how it starts, the second birth takes a lifetime to be complete. Once again, we parents face environmental responsibility: It is our job to provide an environment where the rebirth of our children can begin and where their first steps, not just as our children but as *God's* children, can take place in safety, with instruction and encouragement.

When I picture our job as the spiritual leaders in our family, I picture an old-fashioned scale, the kind the Egyptians used for making accurate measurements. Two containers are hung from a balance beam, one on each side. When the measurement is exact, the plates are even, perfectly balanced. But when they get out of balance, the one with extra weight sinks.

As we think of the spiritual growth of our children, we can think of the two plates containing legalism and license. When we are too legalistic, our parenting style involves too many rules and regulations about spiritual growth, and the scale sinks to the legalism side. On the other hand, if we become careless and do not offer enough guidance or set down enough rules, then the balance falls to the license side. What is it, then, that we can put into each side of the scale to help keep it balanced? I find it helpful to think of putting *freedom* into the legalism side and putting *example* into the license side.

For many Christian parents the risk of legalism is greater than the risk of license. This is not because we really believe in salvation by works. Nor is it that we consciously want to manipulate our children. We love them. But we can be so anxious for them to grow spiritually that we impose growth on them. Or we try to. We cannot actually impose spiritual growth on our children any more than we can impose physical growth. Growth comes from within and in its own time. When we try to rush growth or force our children to wear spiritual clothes that do not fit, we run the risk of trying to play God in our children's lives.

When Jesus told Nicodemus that he needed to be born again, he added this observation about the process: "The Spirit gives birth to spirit. . . . The wind blows wherever it pleases. You hear its sound, but you cannot tell where it comes from or where it is going. So it is with everyone born of the Spirit" (Jn 3:6-8). There is a supreme mystery to spiritual growth. We can hear the "sound" of it, but we do not always know what causes it or where it will lead.

This mystery is sometimes hard for Christian parents to accept. We hear about little Stevie who "asked Jesus into his heart" when he was three. Or eight-year-old Linda who has memorized the whole book of Romans. Or Randy, the high-school junior who is spending his summer on a missions project. What's wrong with my child, who doesn't like to go to Sunday school? And so we say, "Child, you have to go to church and Sunday school." "You cannot go out to play until we have finished our family Bible reading and prayers." "You must give ten per cent of your babysitting money to the church."

And what does the unwilling child hear? That God will love her more if she goes to church and Sunday school. That praying is always more important than playing. And that God needs her hard-earned money.

That may sound harsh, and there can be good reasons for parents having all of those rules, but we need to be very honest with ourselves about the potential for legalism in our Christian families. We need to ask ourselves why we have the rules we have, and what those rules are communicating about God to our children. Sometimes we force our children into spiritual molds because of peer pressure in our own lives. "What will people think?" Sometimes we do it because we are worried and cannot wait for God to give growth. "My child is in junior high and hasn't read through the Bible yet." And sometimes, when we think we are acting in love, our children hear, in fact, just a few more reasons why we don't accept them as they are.

All of this legalism is in sharp contrast to the father who stood in the middle of the road waiting to embrace his wayward son, even before the son confessed or made reparations (Lk 15:11-31). It is in sharp contrast to the message of the gospel that God in his sovereign grace will save us because he loves us and not because we earn his favor.

In his letter to the Galatians, Paul addresses the question of whether or not Christians should follow the Jewish law of circumcision. While the issues of legalism in our society do not involve the rite of circumcision, I believe we can apply what Paul says to some of the extraneous demands and expectations we put on ourselves and on our children. Commenting on Galatians 6:11-18, Eugene Peterson gives the following paraphrase:

"For my part, I am going to boast in nothing but the cross of our Lord Jesus Christ, by which the world is crucified to me and I to the world, setting me free from the stifling atmosphere of pleasing others and fitting into the little patterns they dictate. Can't you see the central issue in all this? It is not what you and I do—submit to circumcision, reject circumcision—it is what God is doing, and he is creating a new thing, a free life!" *(Traveling Light,* IVP, 1982, p. 187)

If we are expecting anything of ourselves or our children which is not a clear instruction in Scripture, then we need to ask ourselves if we are submitting to something besides the freedom Jesus gives us. The important thing is not following a set of rules, or meeting the expectations of others, but growing in our knowledge of God and in our experience of his love and grace. When our children balk at something which we consider a necessary part of their spiritual experience, we do well to ask ourselves if Scripture confirms our assumption and if the activity which is causing problems really does draw our children closer to God's grace.

God *is* creating spiritual life in our children. He *is* re-birthing them.

We can enhance this process, but we cannot initiate it, and we cannot hurry it. And we dare not hamper it by putting legalistic weights in our children's lives.

But the other side of the balance is important too. If we become too cautious out of fear of legalism, or too careless out of laziness, we may give way to license. Out of spiritual ignorance, or out of blatant sinfulness, our children may become spiritual dwarfs. The way to avoid this grave danger is not by borrowing rules from the legalism side of the scale, but by adding your own clear example to the danger-of-license side.

I asked some friends of mine, a couple who grew up in Christian homes, what their parents had done that helped them most in their own spiritual growth. Without hesitation, they both said, "They gave us their example." The husband, David, said that he watched his father express his faith with gentleness and with the attitude of a servant. Dave's dad was consistent in living out his convictions. When it was hard to do that, he involved his family in his struggle, asking them for their perspective and help. By his parents' example, Dave learned that God loved him. He says that his parents were always interested in him and in his activities. "I didn't realize how unusual this was until I became an adult and met people who didn't grow up with parents like that."

Dave's reflections on his parents remind me of George MacDonald's appreciation for his own father. MacDonald's biographer writes about George's love for his father and adds the comment, "Here was a man one might, in his wildest dreams, dare to *hope* that God resembled!" (Michael Phillips, *George MacDonald, Scotland's Beloved Storyteller,* Bethany House, 1987, p. 87). What a compliment to his father!

Paul, in writing to his own spiritual children, told them that it was appropriate that he be their example. In fact, he dared to say, "I urge you to imitate me" (1 Cor 4:16). The author of Hebrews wrote, "We do not want you to become lazy, but to imitate those who through faith and patience inherit what has been promised" (Heb 6:12).

Would you want your children to imitate you? I certainly don't always want that! But I am convinced that it is our example, rather than our rules, which will protect our children from license. Our children need to see us love Jesus, not because he always gives us what we want, but because he is King. They need to see us read the Bible, not because we always want to, but because it is God's Word. They need to see us living by God's rules, not because our obedience makes God love us more, but because they are his rules and they are good for us.

They need to see and to experience from us extravagant love and generous grace because God the Father is extravagantly loving and gracious. They need to see us forgive others because God forgives us. They need to see us be creative in solving our problems because God does not use exactly the same solution twice. They need to see us exercise a living faith, based on today's realities, not on outdated assumptions.

God is alive. We want our children to live in him. They are most likely to find life in him if they see him living in us.

I would consider this call to be a spiritual example to my children an utter absurdity if it were not for the opportunity to have a daily quiet time. Every believer has a way to grow and stay in the faith that helps him better than other ways. The way that helps me the most is to be able to come before God on a daily basis to read his Word and to verbalize my needs and concerns to him in prayer.

In fact, I believe that having a quiet time is probably my most important job as a parent. It keeps all the other responsibilities in perspective. It is the place where I can remember that God is in control, that he loves me and loves my children, and that he has certain priorities for our family. There have been many days over the years when I have not had a quiet time, but the pattern of meeting with God first thing in the morning is critical to my own growth and to the example I try to give my children.

This is why my favorite gift from Bob is not the gold necklace (which I love!) or my watch (which I wear every day), but it is the gift he gave me of the first forty-five minutes of every day in our early years of parenting.

Almost immediately after we brought Dorie home from the hospital, I found out that I could not concentrate with her in the same room. Even the quiet coos of a happy baby were too much for me! So Bob decided that he would plan his morning in such a way that he could care for our children while I had my quiet time. Sometimes this meant that we both had to get up earlier in order to fit it in. For years it meant that he was the chief cook and bottlewasher for breakfast. And, when Dorie and Elisa became toddlers, it meant that they had their own plastic razors so that they could shave with Daddy.

It also meant that I had to find a comfortable spot behind a closed door, and that I went through many pairs of very effective earplugs! But it was all worth the effort. I have no doubt that my faith is stronger and my mothering more loving because of those hours Bob gave me. Leading our children toward spiritual growth means, first of all, that we are growing ourselves.

For Personal Reflection
1. Write one sentence summarizing how you view your responsibility in terms of your children's spiritual life.

What are your greatest strengths in helping you carry out that responsibility?

What does your spouse (or a close friend) do the best to help your children grow spiritually?

2. What do you see as the greatest spiritual need of each of your children at this season in his/her life? What is one thing you, or someone else, can do to help meet that need?

3. If you were to say to your children, "I urge you to imitate me," what spiritual disciplines would they imitate?

4. In what ways do you think your family errs on the side of legalism?

In what ways do you err on the side of license?

If you could make one change in your family's spiritual life, what would it be?

For Group Discussion

1. What influenced you the most to become a Christian? In what ways did your own family of origin help or hinder that process?

2. What "rules," if any, do you think a Christian family should have?

How have you tried to incorporate rules, or lack of rules, into your own family life and spiritual growth?

3. As you think about the example you set for your children, which of the following truths do you think you demonstrate the best? Which would you most like to demonstrate better?

Jesus is King.

The Bible is God's Word.

God calls us to pray.

God requires obedience to his commands.

God loves us.

God forgives us.

God helps us solve our problems.

God is alive and active in the world today.

4. Read 1 Samuel 3. What did Eli do "right" with Samuel? What did he do "wrong" with his sons? What person do you identify with more in this story? Why? In this chapter of Scripture do you recognize a sin to confess? an example to follow? a lesson to learn? Pray for each other.

Chapter 12
Seasons of Marriage and Family Life

I love Christmas. I join with others singing, "Glory to the newborn King!" I love newborn babies. So small and fragile. So helpless and needy. So responsive to the love I want to pour into them. How amazing that God chose to enter the world as a helpless newborn baby.

We don't hear a lot about Jesus' childhood after his birth. What kind of parents were Mary and Joseph? Did Jesus fight with his brothers and sisters? What was their family life like? We can only guess.

I believe that it is not an accident that *adolescence* is the only other part of Jesus' childhood that the Gospels talk about. Jesus was twelve years old when he stayed behind at the temple, upsetting his worried parents (Lk 2:41-50). We don't often think of Jesus as an awkward teenage boy. Yet these years were as much a part of his humanity as his birth, his ministry and his death. Some of us who have parented adolescents might be reassured by a second celebration of Christmas: "Hark the herald angels sing/ Glory to the adolescent king!"

Preschool years and adolescence. Two of the most intense times of parenting. In these times, as at other seasons of parenting, there is a dimension of surprise when we arrive at a new place. When we moved into the teenage years, I remember throwing up my hands in amazement.

"This is exactly what everyone said would happen! Why didn't someone tell me it would be like this?!"

The seasons of life are like that. In the wintertime I can hardly imagine what the trees look like with leaves on them. In the summertime, when I am suffocating my way through a midwestern heat wave, I vow I will never again complain about the cold!

As parents, we would do well to brace ourselves for the seasons of family life.

The birth of a child brings unprecedented changes into a household. This fragile, helpless being can wreak havoc with our routines and expectations. Then come the preschool years, without a doubt the most demanding time for parents, in terms of constant demands on our time and the need for phenomenal physical energy.

School years usher in other demands. How many eleventh-hour science fair projects can you supervise? How many hurt feelings can you touch with love? Then come the adolescent years. Sally Conway, in *Women in Mid-Life Crisis,* says that the lowest point of marital satisfaction usually occurs when there are teenagers living at home (p. 106). And then, suddenly, all is quiet. The living room doesn't get messed up every evening. Dinner can be anytime we want it. Peace at last. Or is it? My friends of the empty nest tell me that the emotions, demands and questions of parenting continue right into our children's adult years.

So how can we maintain our own emotional health, marital well-being and spiritual growth throughout the seasons of parenting? I would like to suggest three areas we need to consider as we weather the seasons of our children's lives. (1) We need to attend to our own physical, emotional and intellectual health. (2) We need to maintain health and partnership in our marriages. (3) We need to keep a careful balance on our "extra-curricular" responsibilities.

I was reminded about the need for parents to take care of their own needs on a recent trip to Philadelphia. As our plane taxied toward the runway, the stewardess demonstrated the use of the overhead oxygen mask, while her colleague described what to do in the "unlikely event" of an emergency. She reminded us that those traveling with young children should put on their own masks first and then help the children with theirs. I have never experienced an "unlikely event" in the air, but I imagine my instinct would be just the opposite of the stewardess's instructions. I would want to help my children first, and then put on my own mask. In a full-fledged emergency, I could be without oxygen myself and unable to help my children at all.

When "unlikely events" (and those not so unlikely!) occur in our family, the same phenomenon happens. If my oxygen supply is low, if I am emotionally, physically or spiritually drained, then I cannot help Dorie and Elisa the way I would like to. It has taken years of experimenting and failure to begin to recognize how much sleep I need, how much time alone I need, how much support from friends I need, and how much love from Bob is necessary for me to be available when emergencies hit. I do not, of course, always have all those needs met. It was years before I started getting enough sleep. There are times when I cannot get alone, and other times when I am lonely. But fatigue, loneliness and burnout should not be the norm for parents.

I am afraid, however, that some parents have accepted a style of parenting that leaves them worn-out, depressed and unable to cope with their children because they cannot get their own needs met. Many women feel guilty whenever they "neglect" their families to take a class, read a book or take a nap. I know of fathers whose fear of failure at work keeps them so long at the office that when they come home they can do little but flop down in front of the television. Sometimes mothers and fathers have to work extra hours, even when they would prefer not to, in order to help pay off the mortgage on an expensive home.

Everything in me says "This ought not to be so!" If we are neglecting our own health to such an extent that it handicaps our parenting ability, then we are, once again, believing the Enemy's lies. Perhaps we are believing the lie that if we love our children we will *always* be available to them. Perhaps we are believing the lie that success at work (or in ministry) is more important than success at home. Or perhaps we are believing that parental love is best communicated through things, accomplishments or activities.

If, on the other hand, we choose to believe the truth, then we will believe that "in repentance and rest is your salvation, in quietness and trust is your strength" (Is 30:15). "Unless the LORD builds the house, its builders labor in vain. . . . In vain you rise early and stay up late, toiling for food to eat, for he grants sleep to those he loves" (Ps 127:1-2). He "satisfies your desires with good things. . . . As a father has compassion on his children, so the LORD has compassion on those who fear him; for he knows how we are formed, he remembers that we are dust" (Ps 103:5, 13-14).

When Jesus came to visit, his friend Martha was "distracted by all the preparations that had to be made." Jesus, Scripture tells us, reprimanded her. "Martha, Martha," the Lord answered, "you are worried and upset about many things but only one thing is needed" (Lk 10:40-

41). Jesus, of course, was talking about spending time with him, which is essential for every mother and father. But when I couple Jesus' perspective with scriptural teaching on rest and trust, I am reminded that it is not neglect when I retreat to be quiet, close my door to sleep, or go out to be refreshed. Far from being neglect, these times are investments which will pay dividends to my children.

The second area where we need to be strong to weather the changing seasons of parenthood is in our marriage relationships. But, first, a word about single parenting. God's intent is that children have mothers and fathers, not just for conception but for all of their childhood years. Single parents in our society face a special challenge to look for creative and redemptive ways to accommodate the loss of regular, two-parent involvement with their children.

I feel sure that if Scripture were written today, God would include words of reminder to us to take special care of single parents, as he told those in biblical times to take special care of widows. He is still Creator and Redeemer. He wants to help us. He wants us to help one another. We need to receive and to give special grace and help in light of the special needs of single parents.

But those of us who are raising children in two-parent families also have special needs. And one of those needs is the nurturing of our marriages. There are dozens of reasons why we need to do this. Most of us begin our marriages as a partnership, give birth and raise our family, and then return to that same partnership. If it has not been nurtured, as we have been busy with our children, then there will be little to return to. Most of us, furthermore, have unique and different gifts to offer our children. I am delighted that Bob and I are different, so that Elisa and Dorie can benefit from our differing gifts and temperaments. And because there are two of us, we can help each other in our weaknesses. "Two are better than one, because they have a good return for their work: If one falls down, his friend can help him up" (Eccl 4:9-10).

Before we had children, I thought that one of the highest values for parents would be absolute consistency in their instruction of their children. They would always echo one another in what they said to their children. I still believe that consistency in values is very important. But if Bob and I disagree about a minor issue, or if one of us is strong at a moment when the other is weak, that's just all the more reason to be thankful that there are two of us!

This brings to mind a time when Dorie was about three years old. At a moment of utter frustration, when she was very mad at me, she looked up at me and shouted, "Shut up!" "Oh, Dorie," I quickly countered in my most stern voice, "we do *not* say 'Shut up!' in our family!"

Later in the week, Bob was taking Dorie somewhere in the car. As he was making his way through heavy traffic, Dorie was chattering away in her best motor-mouth fashion. After several unsuccessful attempts to get her to be quiet, Bob finally said, "Dorie, would you shut up!"

When Dorie (of course) reported the interchange at dinner, we all had a good laugh. We could afford to laugh, because none of us felt that we needed to be perfect all the time. We have each other to help when we are weak.

The importance of maintaining a good marriage throughout the parenting years can hardly be overstated.

In *How to Really Love Your Child*, Ross Campbell goes so far as to say, "The most important relationship in the family is the marital relationship. It takes primacy over all others including the parent-child relationship. Both the quality of the parent-child bond and the child's security are largely dependent on the quality of the marital bond. So you can see why it is important to assure the best possible relationship between wife and husband before seriously attempting to relate to our child in more positive ways" (p. 19).

It is the marriage relationship, however, which is one of the most threatened by today's societal pressures. Many experts believe, furthermore, that the role of men is of utmost importance in the husband-wife relationship as well as in the parent-child relationship, and that it is the role of men which has been most damaged by these pressures. Augustus Napier writes in *The Fragile Bond* that "the hardest work in changing habitual patterns in marriage must be done by men" (p. 338).

"Fathers," says Ross Campbell, "the initiative must be ours" *(How to Really Love Your Child,* p. 23). The current trend toward more father-involvement in parenting is good, but men have a long road ahead to overcome the historical precedent of non-involvement with their families. One survey in 1975 said that the average American child aged two to twelve saw his or her father for 12½ minutes a day. These children from 1975 will be parents soon. It will take strong convictions for them to unlearn that pattern.

It will also take creativity and a clear sense of priorities. As I have observed fathers taking a more active role in their children's lives, I see them struggling with how to give adequate time to their wives, also, and how to maintain appropriate productivity at work. Fathers do not have an easy task. And as more and more women are entering the work force, the task of nurturing spouses and children is becoming more and more difficult for both mothers and fathers.

But throughout history, God has called upon his people to do difficult jobs. His Word has never been, "Watch out for societal pressures and just do the best you can." Rather, he tells us, "Endure hardship with us like a good soldier of Christ Jesus. No one serving as a soldier gets involved in civilian affairs—he wants to please his commanding officer" (2 Tim 2:3-4). Every husband and wife, every mother and father, will need to decide personally what this means in their own families, but we need much support to do this. I meet regularly for Bible study with a group of women who help me apply Scripture to the particular, current demands of my life. Bob and I talk daily about our own needs and the needs of our children. We pray regularly for God's grace to meet those needs.

Over the years we have seen God's grace expressed in many, many different ways. Our own needs have varied from season to season and the expression of God's love has varied so that we can see and enjoy his presence in our lives in many different ways.

Obedience, too, has looked different in different seasons. At some seasons we have had to retreat to spend a lot of time with our children. At other seasons we have been freer to be involved in more of the "busyness" of life. As much as I love variety in my life, sometimes I find it difficult to move from season to season. Just when I think I have my life organized, something changes! This has been especially difficult for me in the area of "extracurricular activities."

Most Christian parents, I find, have a hard time balancing the needs of their families with the needs they see outside. We are torn between family, work, church, fun and ministry, to name just a few. I can remember many nights coming home late from a church meeting only to find that Dorie or Elisa still needed me for something before I could go to bed. I didn't like to admit it, but I felt torn between "the Lord's work" and my family. What an unfair position for God to put me in!

But God did not put me there. I put myself there. Scriptural teaching on marriage and family versus ministry and service makes it clear that marriage qualifies ministry, ministry does not qualify marriage.

This does not mean that family always takes precedence over ministry and service. It is certainly not that simple. But Scripture provides a starting point by teaching that those who minister are to have strong family relationships. If they don't, they are not to minister

(1 Tim 3:1-13). In fact, if the relationship between husband and wife is broken, even prayer ministry is affected. "You flood the LORD's altar with tears. You weep and wail because he no longer pays attention to your offerings or accepts them with pleasure from your hands. You ask, 'Why?' It is because the LORD is acting as the witness between you and the wife of your youth, because you have broken faith with her, though she is your partner, the wife of your marriage covenant" (Mal 2:13-14). God does not accept our excuses for neglecting our own families for the sake of work, ministry and community service.

Again, this certainly does not mean that I always place my family's needs before every other opportunity. What it means is that we need to have very sharply tuned antennae to signals from our spouse or children that their needs are being unmet on a regular basis.

This is especially true during the preschool years and during the adolescent years. In fact, Napier comments that "with the possible exception of the birth of children, at no time in the family life cycle are fathers more needed than during this era [of adolescence]." He emphasizes this further: "The hidden agenda in the families of adolescents is often father's lack of involvement with parenting. While mothers may be able to parent young children alone, adolescents are another matter" (p. 333).

As a mother, I have felt that I needed to pull back from some of my outside activities during these teen years in much the same way I needed to pull back during the preschool years. The need for physical presence is, of course, not as strong as our children get older, but the need for emotional support increases, especially during the adolescent years. I found, to my surprise, that I needed more time alone, more time of restoration, because the emotional drain was as exhausting to me in the teen years as getting up at night had been during the preschool years! A baby screams out his needs and demands. The needs of an adolescent are much more subtle. We need to be alert to both the needs themselves and the opportunities to meet those needs in unobtrusive ways. This means giving the children extra time at this season of life.

The seasons of our children's lives are not unlike the seasons of a garden. In the spring, I do lots of hard work turning the soil and planting the new seedlings. During the growing months, the work of weeding and pruning goes on at a regular pace. Then in the fall (my garden's adolescence?), there is a period of more intense work as I harvest, turn over the soil and get ready to leave my garden for a while.

These seasons of my garden do not surprise me. I am not discouraged when the tomato plants are not laden with fruit in the spring. I don't expect everything I try to be successful. I certainly don't expect everything to be fun. But one of the things I like about gardening is the variety, the creativity, the changing seasons.

And part of what I like about parenting is meeting the challenges that each new season brings.

For Personal Reflection

1. As you reflect on your life as a parent, which "season" have you enjoyed the most? What do you remember about how your own parents related to you during that season of your childhood? What part did your spouse have in the season you enjoyed the most?

2. Which of the following problems occur frequently in your own life when you are not taking adequate care of your emotional, spiritual or physical health?

depression	loneliness	spiritual dryness
burnout	self-pity	fatigue
carelessness	controlling attitude	

Describe a time recently when you found yourself experiencing one of these symptoms. Looking back with the benefit of hindsight, what was the main underlying problem? How did you end up in depression or whatever? What would you do differently another time?

What specific things could your spouse do to help you when you feel like that?

If you are a single parent, how could a friend or another family member help you? Does that person know of your need or interest in help?

3. Read Luke 10:38-42. Close your eyes and picture yourself in Mary and Martha's home. If you had been there, visiting for a meal, what would you have been doing during this interchange? Who do you identify with more, Mary or Martha? What might Jesus have said to you? How can you apply his words to your family situation right now?

4. Considering your own marriage relationship, to what extent does your spouse meet your needs?

   a great deal   adequately   minimally   not at all

To what extent do you meet your spouse's needs?

   a great deal   adequately   minimally   not at all

Compare your answers. Are there needs in your own life which you think your spouse could be meeting? Listen carefully to each other.

For Group Discussion
1. At what season of life did your own parents do the best job of parenting you? What was that season like for you as a child?

2. Ross Campbell says that a strong marriage relationship is good for our children. What specific things do you do to keep your own relationship strong? What evidence have you seen that this is helpful to your children?

3. Paul wrote to Timothy: "Give proper recognition to those widows who are really in need" (1 Tim 5:3). In what ways are widows similar (or dissimilar) to single parents today? What are the greatest needs of single parents? What are the responsibilities of the Christian community to meet those needs? What can single parents do to meet their needs themselves?

4. Jeremiah 29:4-14 includes God's instructions and promises to the Israelites when they were in exile in Babylon. They were to "build houses and settle down; plant gardens. . . . Marry and have sons and daughters." Write out one or two sentences which you think God might say to us as we live in spiritual exile in the twentieth century. Read your sentences to one another.

Epilog

I made the conscious decision to write in the midst of life. It is easy to forget the pain and frustration of our failures. (It is often a good thing that we forget!) But it is a matter of integrity for me that I not pontificate about parenting from the safety and immunity of history. I will remember my successes with relish. By the grace of God, my failures will be redeemed. I decided to write while I am still experiencing both the failures and the successes.

A few weeks ago, I challenged that decision. I almost threw out the manuscript in the face of my own parenting failures. It was a Tuesday, trash day on our street, so it would have been easy. But then God reminded me that he is in charge. Whether or not I feel like a failure on any particular day has little to do with whether or not he wants me to write. He entered my life that day in a moment of pain and said, "I love you."

And so I have written, not because I am always successful, but because he loves me. He redeems our failures and gives us the privilege of serving him.

As I finish this manuscript I find my friend Joseph coming to mind. Joseph spoke some of my favorite words of Scripture. The product of a dysfunctional family himself, the victim of incredible sibling rivalry, and an exile who had not seen his family for at least two decades, Joseph was able to say to his brothers, "I am your brother Joseph, the one you sold into Egypt! And now, do not be distressed and do not be angry with yourselves for selling me here, because it was to save lives that God sent me ahead of you. . . . Don't be afraid. . . . You intended to harm me, but God intended it for good to accomplish what is now being done, the saving of many lives" (Gen 45:4-5; 50:19-20).

What a commentary on God's grace and forgiveness! Satan intends to bring evil and destruction into our families. But God will take even what was intended to harm us and bring good from it. There is no evil beyond his redemption. The good that he has begun in our families, he will complete. His purposes for us will be fulfilled. Amen!

Suggested Reading

Beattie, Melody. *Codependent No More.* New York: Harper & Row, 1987.

Berry, Carmen. *When Helping You Is Hurting Me.* San Francisco: Harper & Row, 1988.

Campbell, D. Ross. *How to Really Love Your Child.* Wheaton, Ill.: Victor Books, 1977.

—————. *How to Really Love Your Teenager.* Wheaton, Ill.: Victor Books, , 1982.

Cline, Foster, and Jim Fay. *Parenting with Love and Logic.* Colorado Springs, Colo.: Nav-Press, 1990.

Conway, Jim and Sally. *Women in Mid-Life Crisis.* Wheaton, Ill.: Tyndale House, 1983.

Crabb, Larry. *Inside Out.* Colorado Springs, Colo.: NavPress, 1988.

Dobson, James. *Hide or Seek.* Old Tappan, N.J.: Revell, 1974.

—————. *Parenting Isn't for Cowards.* Waco, Tex.: Word, 1987.

—————. *The Strong-Willed Child.* Wheaton, Ill.: Tyndale House, 1985.

Faber, Adele, and Elaine Mazlish. *How to Talk So Kids Will Listen.* New York: Avon, 1980.

Field, David. *Family Personalities.* Eugene, Ore.: Harvest House, 1988.

Fryling, Alice and Robert. *A Handbook for Married Couples.* Downers Grove, Ill.: IVP, 1984.

Kuykendall, Carol. *Learning to Let Go.* Grand Rapids, Mich.: Zondervan, 1985.

Leman, Kevin. *The Birth Order Book.* Old Tappan, N.J.: Revell, 1984.

Lerner, Harriet. *The Dance of Anger.* New York: Harper & Row, 1985.

—————. *The Dance of Intimacy.* New York: Harper & Row, 1989.

Napier, Augustus. *The Fragile Bond.* New York: Harper & Row, 1988.

Nouwen, Henri. *Lifesigns.* New York: Doubleday, 1989.

Peterson, Eugene. *Growing Up with Your Teenager.* Old Tappan, N.J.: Revell, 1987.

Rohrer, Norman, and S. Philip Sutherland. *Facing Anger.* Minneapolis: Augsburg, 1981.

Seamands, David. *Healing for Damaged Emotions.* Wheaton, Ill.: Victor Books, 1981.

Silvious, Jan. *Please Don't Say You Need Me.* Grand Rapids, Mich.: Zondervan, 1989.

White, John. *Parents in Pain.* Downers Grove, Ill.: IVP, 1979.